T0065444

Pain
Produces
Power

Pain Produces Power

DAILY DEVOTIONAL

Jenny Hill

WESTBOW
PRESS®
A DIVISION OF THOMAS NELSON
& ZONDERVAN

WestBow Press books may be ordered through booksellers or by contacting:

WestBow Press
A Division of Thomas Nelson & Zondervan
1663 Liberty Drive
Bloomington, IN 47403
www.westbowpress.com
844-714-3454

ISBN: 978-1-9736-9307-9 (sc)
ISBN: 978-1-9736-9306-2 (e)

Print information available on the last page.

WestBow Press rev. date: 10/30/2020

The New Is Here

"Therefore, if anyone is in Christ, the new creation has come: The old has gone, the new is here!" 2 Corinthians 5:17 (NIV)

Today is the start of a new life. Everything that has happened in the past is gone. Leave it in the past. Learn from your mistakes last year and allow it to help shape you into the person you were created to be in Christ. This is a year of great blessings. Claim all that God has for you. Be unstoppable this year letting no one or nothing stand in your way. This is your year to recreate yourself as you allow God to hold you in His hands and carefully mold you into something simply beautiful. Give Him all you have, including the ugly stuff and He will give you back beauty. Get excited for the new you in this new year! Happy New Year!

More Than You Could Ask

"Now to Him who is able to do immeasurably more than all we ask or imagine, according to His power that is at work within us, to Him be glory in the church and in Christ Jesus throughout all generations, forever and ever! Amen."
Ephesians 3:20-21 (NIV)

God is all powerful. He is working through you as He fills you with His awesome power to do what He has called you to do. He is blessing you with more than you could ever imagine as you walk with Him in faith. God is opening doors for you that no man can close. You are being exalted by God and He is going to use you mightily in His Kingdom. Get ready for supernatural increase in all areas of your life this year. God is your refuge and He will let nothing overtake you. Continue to thank God and praise His Holy Name!

Few Are Chosen

———◆———

"Then the king told the attendants, 'Tie him hand and foot, and throw him outside, into the darkness, where there will be weeping and gnashing of teeth.' 'For many are invited, but few are chosen." Matthew 22:13-14 (NIV)

When God calls you to Him, it's important to go to Him right away. Don't ignore His invitation to you. Answer His call when He calls you so you are not one of the ones cast out and thrown into outer darkness. He is calling you to Him with His awesome love. He wants to use you in His Kingdom. You are blessed to be chosen by God, but He will not make you answer His call. He gives us freewill to choose. Choose wisely!

Humble Yourself

———⟫◆⟪———

"The greatest among you will be your servant. For those who exalt themselves will be humbled, and those who humble themselves will be exalted." Matthew 23:11-12 (NIV)

When God chooses someone, He molds them into His great servant. He chooses you to use you for His glory. He doesn't choose you because you're better than anyone else. God will humble you if you don't humble yourself. When God humbles you, it doesn't always feel so good. He will humble you in the way He chooses to and that can be a painful process. You don't have to place yourself above anyone. God will lift you up as you humbly serve Him. The greater servant you are, the greater you are in His Kingdom. Work hard for the Lord as you serve His children and God will bless you beyond your wildest dreams!

JANUARY 5ᵀᴴ

The Lord Leads Me

"The Lord is my Shepherd; I shall not want. He maketh me lie down in green pastures: He leadeth me beside the still waters. He restoreth my soul: He leadeth me in the paths of the righteousness for His name's sake." Psalm 23:1-3 (KJV)

The Lord will provide for you as you follow Him. Ask Him for His guidance and be open to listening to Him once He speaks. God will bring you into perfect peace as you follow Him and He will bring you into prosperity as you can handle it. He won't ever give you anything too fast. With every level comes a bigger devil, which is why it's important to follow God's lead instead of jumping ahead too fast. Process is important and without it, you learn nothing. As you follow His lead, take time to spend with Him and He will refresh your soul!

Putting On The New

—◆—

"Do not lie to each other, since you have taken off your old self with its practices and have put on the new self, which is being renewed in knowledge in the image of its Creator." Colossians 3:9-10 (NIV)

You have been given a chance to become new in Christ. Be careful not to fall back into your old ways. Remember that the devil is the father of lies. Since you have chosen God to be your Father, become more like Him. He is the Father of Truth and He is molding you daily. You are being renewed by the knowledge of His Word. Every morning you awake, put on the new man. Do not be deceived by falling back into the traps of the enemy. You are now a child of Truth, so continue to walk in it daily and experience full freedom in Christ!

Do What The Word Says

―――⟫⟨◆⟩⟪―――

"Do not merely listen to the Word, and so deceive yourselves. Do what it says." James 1:22 (NIV)

It's good to fill yourself up daily with God's Word, but it does nothing for you just to listen to the Word. You must also do what the Word says in order to experience a full transformation and freedom. Walking with God is a never-ending process, but it's full of great blessings along the way. We are on a journey Home. Everything you experience will not be easy, but you will learn to trust God more as you walk hand in hand with Him. He's with you and lighting the way for your feet. You can have perfect peace in the storm if you follow God's direction. Listen to the Word and put the Word into action. You will transform into what God has called you to be in the Kingdom!

JANUARY 8TH

What Is Your Sacrifice?

⫸◆⫷

"Put your sword back in its place," Jesus said to him, "for all who draw the sword will die by the sword. Do you think I cannot call on My Father, and He will at once put at My disposal more than twelve legions of angels? But how then would the Scriptures be fulfilled that say it must happen in this way?" Matthew 26:52-54 (NIV)

When Jesus was coming close to His hour of death, Peter pulled out his sword to protect Jesus, but Jesus made it clear to Peter that He could call on God for help if He wanted, but then He would not be fulfilling His destiny. He sacrificed His own life so that He could save us all from darkness and from an eternity in hell. What sacrifice are you willing to make in your life to help save others from eternal death?

Free From Sin

—❖—

"For we know that our old self was crucified with Him so that the body ruled by sin might be done away with, that we should no longer be slaves to sin - because anyone who has died has been set free from sin." Romans 6:6-7 (NIV)

When you accept Christ into your heart, your old self dies daily. You are transforming into the person you were created to be. Before you accepted Christ as your Lord and Savior, you were a slave to sin. You were in bondage and suffered in darkness, but now you are free in Jesus. He has brought you out of darkness and gave you freedom to live in His light. Your old self is no longer. Everyday your flesh is dying as your spirit is growing stronger. You have become new in Christ. Enjoy being free as you do the thing you were created to do!

JANUARY 10TH

Wait On The Lord

———◆———

"Be still before the Lord and wait patiently for Him; do not fret when people succeed in their ways, when they carry out their wicked schemes." Psalm 37:7 (NIV)

Whenever we see people around us coming into prosperity by doing evil, it makes us feel uneasy. It seems unfair that we are living righteous lives, but are struggling to make ends meet. The people who do wicked things to succeed are coming up fast and living abundant lives, but continue in your righteousness. Don't focus on what other people are doing to get ahead. It's not your business. They have to answer to God. You just be still and do what God is calling you to do. God will prosper you in His perfect timing. Trust His process as He prepares you to live a life of prosperity without using sinful ways to get it!

Predestined For Greatness

→•◇•←

"In Him we were also chosen, having been predestined according to the plan of Him who works out everything in conformity with the purpose of His will, in order that we, who were the first to put our hope in Christ, might be for the praise of His glory." Ephesians 1:11-12 (NIV)

God chose you from the beginning of the world to do something specific in His Kingdom. You are not here by mistake. There is something special that God has raised you up to do. He will work all things out for your good to accomplish His will. God is using your trials to strengthen your character for the next dimension in your life. Whenever you are going through difficult times, rejoice because you know that God is only strengthening you through this battle to promote you to the next level!

The Work Of God's Hand

"Yet You, Lord, are our Father. We are the clay, You are the Potter; we are all the work of Your hands." Isaiah 64:8 (NIV)

God is shaping you daily into what He created you for. He has created us all for a specific purpose. Allow Him to show you what your purpose is here on Earth. Everything that you have been through and are going through is working together to mold you. Your current situation is molding you as we speak. Sometimes we think God sends us places to change things because it's our duty as Christians, which is true, but God is also using the place to change and mold you for your special purpose. Keep in mind that God is using the difficult times to strengthen you and shape you for the next dimension as He prepares you for lift off into your destiny!

JANUARY 13TH

Treasure In Earthen Vessels

—◆—

"But we have this treasure in earthen vessels, that the excellency of the power may be of God, and not of us." 2 Corinthians 4:7 (NIV)

God put a treasure within you. As you follow Him closely, you get closer to the treasure. Your flesh weakens as you grow closer to God and your spirit grows stronger. As your spirit grows stronger, the treasure within you reveals itself. Your treasure is your destiny. God reveals your purpose to you as you follow Him. Don't get discouraged if you don't know what your purpose is right away. Be patient as you follow Jesus. Once you start to understand that you are working through God's power and not your own, God will reveal the treasure placed within you. Your treasure is your special purpose. What did God put you on Earth to change?

JANUARY 14TH

God Gave His Only Son

⋙◆⋘

"This is how God showed His love among us: He sent His one and only Son into the world that we might live through Him." 1 John 4:9 (NIV)

God is a loving God. God is love. He became flesh and dwelt among us so that He could be touched by our infirmities. God did not sacrifice His only Son so that we could be miserable. He gave His only Son to save us from a life of pain and darkness. You are a child of God. He came so that you could live a life full of abundance filled with love, perfect peace, joy, and prosperity. He came to give you eternal life in Him. Not a lot of people would be willing to give a child for a world full of sinners, but God gave His only Son to save us all from this evil world. Thank Him daily by sacrificing and living a life led by His Holy Spirit!

A Man After My Own Heart

―――⋙∘⋘―――

"After removing Saul, He made David their king. God testified concerning him: 'I have found David son of Jesse, a man after My own heart; he will do everything I want him to do." Acts 13:22 (NIV)

God removed Saul as king and anointed David to be the new king. No one expected David to be a king at first. He was only a shepherd boy and a musician. How could he be a king? But when God chooses you, there is no one or nothing that can stop you from getting the position God has for you. God chose David because he did everything God wanted him to do no matter how difficult the task was. Why should God choose you for the position? Can God trust you to do great things if He promotes you to the next level?

New Position

"He must increase, but I must decrease." John 3:30 (KJV)

In order for God to lift you up, you have to be willing to play the background. Allow God to take the lead in your life. He will guide you in all that you do. His Holy Spirit will bring you into places you've never been before. Remain teachable as you follow God. Be a good student and along the way, you will acquire all the skills you need to learn so that you can move onto the next level. Everything you experience won't be easy, but understand that you need those experiences to grow. As you follow God, He will mold you. As you follow His lead and do what He asks you to do, He will bless you. When God decides to bless you, He will make you a blessing for someone else. He will shape you into a great leader!

God Is With You In Trouble

"When you pass through the waters, I will be with you and when you pass through the rivers, they will not sweep over you. When you walk through the fire, you will not be burned; the flames will not set you ablaze." Isaiah 43:2 (NIV)

God won't leave you alone if you are His. He'll be with you through the hardest times of your life. He won't allow you to sink when things become too hard. God is with you through everything that threatens your future. He's always near you. Show your gratitude by allowing Him to use you as a vessel to help others out of captivity. God sets you free, but you still have to work hard. It won't be easy, but if you are God's child, He will be with you through it all. He won't leave you alone. Do not fear because the Most High is on your side!

Light Overcomes Darkness

—⟫◆⟪—

"In Him was life, and that life was the light of all mankind. The light shines in the darkness, and the darkness has not overcome it." John 1:4-5 (NIV)

Before coming to Christ, you live in darkness. You are dead in your sins. When Jesus steps into your life, He wakes you up from a deep sleep. He opens your eyes so that you can see the beauty all around you. His light is blinding to you because you are used to living in the dark. He reveals to you all of your sins. At first it doesn't feel so good. It can be overwhelming trying to figure out where to begin in the process of transformation, but God does not leave you without help. He sends His Holy Spirit to you to guide you through each step. God brings you from death in your sins to life in Him!

His Compassion Never Fails

———◆———

"Because of the Lord's great love we are not consumed, for His compassions never fail. They are new every morning; great is Your faithfulness." Lamentations 3:22-23 (NIV)

There will be times you fail at things and it's ok. No one is perfect. You get stronger and wiser from failing if you choose to learn from your failures. God won't allow His children to drown. It doesn't matter if you fail sometimes, what matters is how you get back up and that you put all you have into the purpose God has called you to. If you fall, God will pick you back up, dust you off, and give you the opportunity to try it again because of His great compassion. Every morning God allows you to start fresh. Yesterday is gone. Today, you get to recreate yourself and do things differently!

Rest From Your Labor

<hr/>

"Then I heard a voice from Heaven say, 'Write this: Blessed are the dead who die in the Lord from now on.' 'Yes,' says the Spirit, 'they will rest from their labor, for their deeds will follow them." Revelation 14:13 (NIV)

When your loved ones pass away, it can be a very difficult time. Although it hurts, we have to remember that they are at peace. They no longer labor here on Earth. They are resting peacefully with our Heavenly Father. Celebrate your loved ones life and the fact that they made it Home. We will see each other again someday. Until then, know that your dead loved ones are still around in spirit cheering you on in your life. They are angels watching over us until our time is up!

Be Strong And Courageous

"Be strong and courageous. Do not be afraid or terrified because of them, for the Lord your God goes with you; He will never leave you nor forsake you." Deuteronomy 31:6 (NIV)

When the enemy rises up against you, continue to stay strong in the Lord. God is with you through whatever you are going through. He will not allow the enemy to overtake you. Do not fear the enemy or his attacks. God will use everything that the enemy used to hurt you, then turn it around and use it for your good. God will never leave you alone through the hardest times of your life. He is fighting the good fight with you and through you!

You Have Been Called

"And the God of all grace, who called you to His eternal glory in Christ, after you have suffered a little while, will Himself restore you and make you strong, firm and steadfast." 1 Peter 5:10 (NIV)

When God calls you, He will protect you from any evil. You may experience hardship, but He will go through it with you. God will allow you to go through the fire, but as you go through it, He will burn away the things that are no longer needed for the next level. After you suffer through hardships, you will be strengthened. You will be immovable. When the enemy comes up against you again, you'll be more prepared for his attack. The enemy won't overtake you this time. Stand firmly in the Lord. Trust Him because all things work together for the good of those who love God!

JANUARY 23RD

No Weapon Shall Prosper

⟾◆⟸

"No weapon that is formed against thee shall prosper; and every tongue that shall rise against thee in judgement thou shalt condemn. This is the heritage of the servants of the Lord, and their righteousness is of me, saith the Lord." Isaiah 54:17 (KJV)

God is keeping you as problems or attacks rise up in your life. He won't allow any of your enemies to overtake you. Sometimes God will allow the enemy to attack you so that He can show His power in your problem. You and people around you will know it had to be God who brought you through the attack. The stronger the attack is in your life, the stronger God's power will be in your life. His strength is made perfect in your weakness!

Forgive One Another

―――◦◦――――

"Bear with each other and forgive one another if any of you has a grievance against someone. Forgive as the Lord forgave you." Colossians 3:13 (NIV)

Your family is a very important part of your life. There will be times you don't agree with one another about certain issues that come up. If an argument or disagreement arises between your family, quickly make amends with that person. Forgive them like the Lord forgives you. If you don't forgive them, the devil takes foothold in your life. A spirit of division may spread if you don't make amends with that person. You never want to have any regrets about the last time you saw that person. Treat your loved ones like it is your last time seeing them because you never know when the last time you see them will be!

Win As Many As Possible

"Though I am free and belong to no one, I have made myself a slave to everyone, to win as many as possible." 1 Corinthians 9:19 (NIV)

When you are a child of God, you are free from everyone and everything. You are no one's slave, but it's important to serve others around you in order to bring others to Jesus Christ. Once other people see how free you are in Christ and how you live your life, it will motivate them to follow Jesus themselves. Eventually you will help save many souls by helping to bring them into the Kingdom. As you are serving God, He will guide you and provide all that you need as you do what He has called you to do!

JANUARY 26TH

Gentle Answers

⟨⟩

A gentle answer turns away wrath, but a harsh word stirs up anger." Proverbs 15:1 (NIV)

Whenever conflict rises up between you and someone else, remain calm. Do not fall into the traps of the enemy by getting upset and engaging in an argument with the other person. You never know what someone else is going through. Some people respond in anger whenever they are hurting deep down inside. The next time the enemy tries using someone to stir up the anger within you, keep still and speak gently toward the other person. Remember not to fight back with the other person, fight the devil using that person to hurt you!

Headless Family

———❖———

"Religion that God our Father accepts as pure and faultless is this: to look after orphans and widows in their distress and to keep oneself from being polluted by the world." James 1:27 (NIV)

There are many wives and children who are left behind. The husband and father may leave or pass on from this physical world. It's important to make sure that the widow and orphan are cared for. If not, it's a strong possibility that the world will come in and destroy all that they have left. If there is no head or leader, it is easier for the enemy to take down the family. Be sure to protect and cover the family who is left behind without the head or leader of their family. God knows your sacrifice as you help this headless family!

Unity Through Peace

⤏◈⤎

"Make every effort to keep the unity of the Spirit through the bond of peace." Ephesians 4:3 (NIV)

It won't always be easy, but it's so important to stay in peace with one another. Unity between you and others is crucial. You get further along in life when you do things as a team. If there is no peace between you and others, there will be no team. Things will become harder if you have no one behind you to help support you and if you don't help support them. If you wrong someone, quickly admit it and ask for their forgiveness. The person may not forgive you right away, but know that you did all you could do on your part to make peace between you and the other person. The more unity you have, the more strength you will have to accomplish big things in the Kingdom!

I Will Rise

—⟫◆⟪—

"Do not gloat over me, my enemy! Though I have fallen, I will rise. Though I sit in darkness, the Lord will be my light."
Micah 7:8 (NIV)

Do not fall into darkness if you trip or stumble over any obstacle. No one is perfect on this earth. Do not allow anyone else's judgement make you feel worse about a situation then you already feel. You have God's grace and mercy being poured out over your life. The enemy may feel good about you stumbling, but you know that God will not allow your enemies to have victory over you. The Lord is your light guiding you out of any darkness, allowing you to see your way back out of the dark. God forgives you for your sins so forgive yourself. You are not a warrior because you win all the time. You are a warrior because you stand up to the fight.

God Is Watching Over Us

—◇—

"It was also called Mizpah, because he said, 'May the Lord keep watch between you and me when we are away from each other." Genesis 31:49 (NIV)

If you're not always able to be with your family, it's ok. Do not worry yourself to death about your family and their well-being. God has His hand on you and them. Mizpah is Hebrew for watchtower. God is the watchtower because He keeps His eye on you. God is protecting you and your family. He is keeping you and your family safe from harm. Continue doing the best that you can do in your own life and allow them to do the same. Build a foundation that you and your family can stand firmly on. When you reunite with your family, it will be with great joy because of all your accomplishments. Work hard to grow a great empire for you and your family.

Sincere Love

—=>◆<=—

"Love must be sincere. Hate what is evil; cling to what is good." Romans 12:9 (NIV)

You will have all kinds of different people enter into your life at different seasons in your life. Be aware of who you have around you and who you are keeping in your life. Some people are supposed to be in your life for only a season and that's ok. Don't try forcing anybody to stay that isn't supposed to stay. The love will not be sincere if you force something to be what it isn't. Keep your eyes open. Do not close them to any evil. You cannot pretend that you don't see or feel evil coming from someone. Stay clear of any evil and hold onto all that is good. You will know when you have sincere love enter into your life. Be grateful for real genuine love.

Division Leads to Destruction

———◆———

"Jesus knew their thoughts and said to them: 'Any kingdom divided against itself will be ruined, and a house divided against itself will fall." Luke 11:17 (NIV)

When you are coming into new levels in your life, new devils come to destroy you. Satan will send a demonic attack against you and your family. Satan will send a spirit of division to divide you from them. If the devil can divide you and your family, it becomes easier for him to destroy you. He will isolate you from your family so that he can attack your mind causing bitterness. Satan will try to divide and conquer you all. After he causes division, it's easier for Satan to ruin and destroy your family. Do everything you can possibly do on your part to keep the peace and the devil will eventually flee.

FEBRUARY 2ND

Do Not Fall Into Fear

⇒◆⇐

"I will not fear though tens of thousands assail me on every side." Psalm 3:6 (NIV)

When you rise up and move into a new level in your life, the devil will attack you harder. Whenever there is more blessing in your life, there will be more persecution. Everytime you break into a new level, expect a new devil to attack you. Do not fear the enemy or his attacks on you. Stay focused so you can reach your destination. When you are attacked on all sides in your life, don't get discouraged. Get excited instead because it only means that you are closer to your destiny than you have ever been before. You are very valuable in the Kingdom and the devil will do whatever it takes to stop you. He will throw all he can at you, but God is your refuge. He will not allow you to drown.

God's Perfect Timing

―――◆◆◆◆―――

"He has made everything beautiful in its time. He has also set eternity in the human heart; yet no one can fathom what God has done from beginning to end." Ecclesiastes 3:11 (NIV)

God has created each and every one of His children for a special purpose. Your journey won't look like anyone else's journey. Some of us struggle in the first half of our lives, but the struggle is what makes you stronger and wiser for the thing you were created to do on Earth. It doesn't matter how you start because God has a season for everything. The second half of your life will be better than the first half of your life. You are coming into your season and there is no devil in Hell that will stop what God has prepared for you. God has prepared something beautiful for you. He has given you eternity with Him. Remain grateful to Him.

FEBRUARY 4ᵀᴴ

Receive Your Crown

———◆———

"Blessed is the one who perseveres under trial because, having stood the test, that person will receive the crown of life that the Lord has promised to those who love Him." James 1:12 (NIV)

Difficult times are going to rise up in your life. There is no way to avoid it. You will feel like giving up sometimes, but you can't quit. Continue moving forward even when trouble surrounds you. You will be blessed for rising above all your obstacles. If you can pass the test that comes up in your life, God will give you the crown of life. He will bless you and richly reward you for continuing to soar through the storms that rise up in your life. Fight for your crown.

FEBRUARY 5TH

Your Eye Is The Lamp

⟶◆⟵

"The eye is the lamp of the body. If your eyes are healthy, your whole body will be full of light. But if your eyes are unhealthy, your whole body will be full of darkness. If then the light within you is darkness, how great is that darkness!" Matthew 6:22-23 (NIV)

Be careful of the activities you engage in. Keep yourself clean and your vision clear. You hold God's light within you. The light God has given you is not only for you to see your way more clearly, but He has filled you with His light so that you can also help others find their way out of darkness. You have been given God's light to light up dark places. Darkness cannot overcome the light God has placed within you. Be sure to shine your light brightly everywhere you go in this world.

FEBRUARY 6TH

Gain Understanding From God

⋘◆⋙

"Where were you when I laid the Earth's foundation? Tell Me, if you understand. Who marked off its dimensions? Surely you know! Who stretched a measuring line across it? On what were its footing set, or who laid its cornerstone - while the morning stars sang together and all the angels shouted for joy?" Job 38:4-7 (NIV)

You may have many questions for God in your life that you don't understand. God is the author of your story. He knows all things. You only see pieces of your story. You don't understand why certain things are happening in your life. You are God's child so you have nothing to worry about. Parts of your life will seem confusing or painful at times, but know that God has a perfect plan for your life. Everything you are going through will be used for your good.

FEBRUARY 7TH

Safe In His Dwelling

—⊰◆⊱—

"For in the day of trouble He will keep me safe in His dwelling; He will hide me in the shelter of His sacred tent and set me high upon a rock." Psalm 27:5 (NIV)

No one living here on this earth is perfect. When trouble rises up you may not always make the best decisions, but God is your refuge. He is keeping you close to Him and He will not allow any harm to come to you. God will cover you underneath His wings, hiding you away from the enemy. Trouble will come sometimes, but allow God to strengthen you through these trials. You have to continue fighting your way up and God will exalt you at the right time. He will set you high on top of your mountain as you conquer whatever threatens your future.

Anchor For The Soul

"We have this hope as an anchor for the soul, firm and secure. It enters the inner sanctuary behind the curtain, where our forerunner, Jesus, has entered on our behalf. He has become a high priest forever, in the order of Melchizedek." Hebrews 6:19-20 (NIV)

God does not allow His children to be carried away in the wind. He is your anchor when storms rise up against you. He is your security when Satan comes at you fast and hard. He will not allow you to drown or be swallowed up when the waters rise. God is holding you in His hands and strengthening you for whatever is coming next in your life. Do not worry about the storms that rise up in your life because Jesus is intervening on your behalf. He is taking care of all your needs as you follow Him.

FEBRUARY 9TH

Christ Died For You

"But God demonstrates His own love for us in this: While we were still sinners, Christ died for us." Romans 5:8 (NIV)

Jesus loves you so much that even though you're a sinner, He died to free you from the darkness of your sins. You don't have to continue feeling trapped in the prison of your past because of the sacrifice Christ made for you. Jesus brings you into the light and freedom of your future. Jesus took the punishment that you should've received for your sins so that you can now move forward freely toward the destination God has waiting just for you. Never question the love God has for you because He gave His only Son to pay the price for you. Continue to show your gratitude toward your God by doing all that He has created you to do. Don't hold back.

Be Fruitful And Increase

"God blessed them and said to them, 'Be fruitful and increase in number; fill the earth and subdue it. Rule over the fish in the sea and the birds in the sky and over every living creature that moves on the ground." Genesis 1:28 (NIV)

God didn't put you on this earth to be miserable or to isolate yourself from others. He wants you to get out into the world. If you isolate yourself, you won't get the chance to change a life. God gives you things to see what you will do with them. If He sees He can trust you to make the most out of what He has given you, then He will bless you with even more. He wants you to grow, prosper, and to have complete joy in the journey He has blessed you to walk. Get out into the world as you allow God to use you as a vessel for His glory.

FEBRUARY 11ᵀᴴ

Love One Another

—◆—

"A new command I give you: Love one another. As I have loved you, so you must love one another." John 13:34 (NIV)

Love is such a powerful thing. You are free because of the love of Christ. He gave up everything to give you everything. Love your neighbor the way Jesus loves you. Do all you can possibly do to make peace wherever you are. If you see your brother or sister down, stick out your hand to help them up. If you see someone struggling, encourage them or comfort them. You never know who you are helping. You could be entertaining an angel or God Himself. Love all people in the name of Jesus Christ.

FEBRUARY 12TH

Working for the Lord

"Whatever you do, work at it with all your heart, as working for the Lord, not for human masters, since you know that you will receive an inheritance from the Lord as a reward. It is the Lord Christ you are serving." Colossians 3:23-24 (NIV)

When you're called by Christ, He puts a passion within you for a certain purpose. As you go after your purpose, make sure you put all you have into it. Don't worry about what others are saying or what they think. Working hard for the Lord is all that matters since it is Him who will reward you in the end. God put a gift within all of us and it is up to you to dig down deep to find out what your gift is. Thank God everyday for the gift or gifts He has given you. Enjoy the journey toward your destination.

Remain Rooted In Jesus Christ

"So then, just as you received Christ Jesus as Lord, continue to live your lives in Him, rooted and built up in Him, strengthened in the faith as you were taught, and overflowing with thankfulness." Colossians 2:6-7 (NIV)

When you were lost in darkness, it felt like you would never have peace and joy again. There are many people who don't find their way out of the dark into the light, but God chose to bring you out of the darkness and to fill you with His love. He filled you with His light. Now that Christ has chosen you, don't turn back. Stay in the arms of the Lord and follow His way. As you remain in the Lord and follow the guidance of His Holy Spirit, He will build you up. The Lord will strengthen you as you follow Him. Be grateful for everything the Lord is doing in your life and He will continue to bless you. The Lord blesses those who remain thankful.

FEBRUARY 14ᵀᴴ

You Are Being Cleansed By God

—◆—

"Come now, let us settle the matter," says the LORD. "Though your sins are like scarlet, they shall be as white as snow; though they are red as crimson, they shall be like wool.'"
Isaiah 1:18 (NKJV)

We are all born sinners. Not one of us is perfect, but God sent His only Son Jesus Christ to take away the sins of the world. Once you accept Christ into your heart, your life will start to change little by little. He cleanses the impurities within you and He transforms you into the person you were created to be. If you backslide, don't be so hard on yourself. Confess your sins and ask for forgiveness. As you grow into the person God created you to be, there will be times that you stumble. Don't allow yourself to give up altogether. Get back up and continue pursuing your purpose. Run after your purpose with everything you have!

FEBRUARY 15TH

God's Precious Thoughts

———◈———

"How precious also are Your thoughts to me, O God! How great is the sum of them. If I should count them, they would be more in number than the sand; When I awake, I am still with You." Psalm 139:17-18 (NKJV)

All of God's children are special to Him. He upholds every single one of His children in His hand. God chose you for something great. He guides you along daily, keeping you safe from harm. His thoughts toward you are numerous. He is using every moment in your life to shape you and to mold you. Nothing will be wasted. God uses your hurts, your downfalls, your happiness, and your victories to make you victorious overall. Keep your eyes on the Lord and trust Him in everything you do.

FEBRUARY 16TH

Remain Hopeful

"For in this hope we were saved. But hope that is seen is no hope at all. Who hopes for what they already have? But if we hope for what we do not yet have, we wait for it patiently."
Romans 8:24-25 (NIV)

You were brought out of darkness into God's light for something special. God has chosen you to achieve something great. Trust in God fully although He cannot be seen. God is a spirit. As you worship Him in spirit and truth, you will feel Him moving through you. Trust God's hand to lead you on. Pray to Him continuously and be patient. Pray and wait for Him to move. As you follow Jesus wherever He leads you, He will exalt you as you remain humble. Put your faith and hope in the Lord. He will uplift you in His perfect timing.

The Lord Is Your Strength

———⊰◈⊱———

"The LORD is my strength and song, And He has become my salvation." Psalm 118:14 (NKJV)

Following Christ will feel great to your spirit when you first come to Him, but as He grows you and builds you up, the process can get a little tough. There will be trials that come to strengthen you. When these trials come, don't be discouraged or afraid. This is all a part of God's plan to strengthen you for the promise. The pressure that falls on you will produce the power you need to accomplish God's will. God uses struggle to strengthen your core. He can't bring you into higher levels until you are prepared to deal with the pressures that come with going to the top. While you're in the midst of a trial, remember that God is your defense. He saved you for something great. He will guide you on this journey to greatness.

FEBRUARY 18TH

Faith Comes By Hearing

"Consequently, faith comes from hearing the message, and the message is heard through the word about Christ." Romans 10:17 (NIV)

You need faith when you choose to follow Jesus Christ on your journey to achieve greatness because things will be up some days and down other days. Jesus is the rock that you will need to stand firmly when you are going through these ups and downs. It may feel a little scary at times, but your faith will allow you to trust Jesus during the process of becoming more like Christ. In order to grow your faith, you need to hear the Word of God. His Word is what will give you wisdom and it will be your guide. God's Word will fill you with the strength you need to stand strong in the fight. God's Word is the light you need to see your way clearly toward the promise.

Remission Of Sins

⟫◆⟪

"For this is My blood of the new testament, which is shed for many for the remission of sins." Matthew 26:28 (KJV)

Jesus Christ was beaten, flogged, and nailed to a cross for you. He took on your punishment to save you from eternal death. Before He gave up His spirit, He said, "It is finished." This means that He has already paid the price for your sins. Stop feeling guilty for the past. It is time to move on. Jesus didn't suffer and die so you could live in darkness. He died to give you freedom from your past and to give you another chance for eternal life. He wants you to have perfect peace and joy. Enjoy your life here on earth and do all that God is calling you to do with a smile on your face. You don't have to be sad or live in darkness anymore. God set you free!

The Memory Of The Righteous

"The memory of the righteous is blessed, But the name of the wicked will rot." Proverbs 10:7 (NKJV)

God brought you into His light so He could use you to accomplish great things here on earth. He is pouring out His favor over you as He blesses all that your hands touch and wherever your feet walk. God will bless every sacrifice you make for His Kingdom. There are wicked people who make it to the top, but all they've accomplished is forgotten. The truth always comes out eventually. What happens in the dark will always be exposed in the light. The wicked will only be remembered for the bad that they've done while on this earth, but you are righteous. The work of your hands and the sacrifices you've made for God's Kingdom will be remembered by many for a long time!

FEBRUARY 21ST

The Lord Gives And Takes Away

———❖———

"And he said: 'Naked I came from my mother's womb, And naked shall I return there. The Lord gave, and the Lord has taken away; Blessed be the name of the Lord.'" Job 1:21 (NKJV)

Once God raises you up, He will start the process of transformation so that He can use you for His glory. As you are being exalted, always remain humble. Remember where your blessings are coming from. Be careful not to fall into pride as you are coming into your purpose. Always remember that it is God who is working through you to achieve greatness. If you become prideful or begin doing things in your own power, God will take everything He gave you away. Sometimes God will take certain things away even when you are following His way, but He will take it away to bless you with more. Trust everything God is doing in your life even when it doesn't make any sense. Don't question God, but trust Him fully.

The Lord Will Exalt You

—✦—

"Therefore humble yourselves under the mighty hand of God, that He may exalt you in due time, casting all your care upon Him, for He cares for you." 1 Peter 5:6-7 (NKJV)

God is bringing you into new levels. As He lifts you up, remain humble and listen to His direction. Be careful of doing things in your own power. After so long, you will tire yourself out. Allow God to work through you and trust Him in the process. If God says no, don't be discouraged because it means He has better for you. Whenever you feel afraid, fearful, doubtful, depressed, or angry, give it all to God. He will lighten your load. He will carry all of your burdens for you. Don't allow the cares of this world to weigh you down. God is working everything out for you right now. Wait patiently for the Lord to move you.

Nothing Can Stop God's Plan

"For the Lord of hosts has purposed, And who will annul it? His hand is stretched out, And who will turn it back?" Isaiah 14:27 (NKJV)

When God calls your name and reaches His hand out to you, don't ignore His call. He has created you for a special purpose and you have been raised up at this very moment to begin your journey. No one can stop the calling on your life. Don't be afraid when your enemies rise up against you. God's plan will not be thwarted. When He speaks a Word it will come to pass. Get ready to enter the next level toward your purpose.

Have Joy In Your Suffering

⟨──◈──⟩

"My brethren, count it all joy when ye fall into divers temptations; Knowing this, that the trying of your faith worketh patience. But let patience have her perfect work, that ye may be perfect and entire, wanting nothing." James 1:2-4 (KJV)

God is shaping you and molding you into the person He created you to be. God is the Potter and you are the clay. He will cut you in places that hurt and press on other places to shape you. Molding can be painful, but when you are experiencing a cutting in your life, be joyful in the suffering. Remember why you are going through certain trials. God is taking and adding the ingredients needed to make you whole so that you can receive His promise. He is producing the power within you to accomplish your mission, but the process can be painful at times. After you've endured the suffering, God will bring you into purpose.

United In Jesus Christ

"Now I plead with you, brethren, by the name of our Lord Jesus Christ, that you all speak the same thing, and that there be no divisions among you, but that you be perfectly joined together in the same mind and in the same judgment." 1 Corinthians 1:10 (NKJV)

There are going to be times when you disagree with one another, but it's more important to keep peace and unity between all who are in Christ. There is strength in numbers. More can be accomplished when there is unity. Be watchful because the enemy hates unity. He will do all he can to cause division among brothers and sisters. When the enemy is successful in dividing people. He will bring a person into isolation. It's dangerous when the enemy is able to isolate a person from the group because he will get inside the person's mind. He will cause the person to become angry, depressed, and hopeless. It's important to make amends as quickly as possible and to remain a united front.

God Called You By Name

"But now, thus says the Lord, who created you, O Jacob, And He who formed you, O Israel: 'Fear not, for I have redeemed you; I have called you by your name; You are Mine.'" Isaiah 43:1 (NKJV)

The Lord chose to redeem you. He saved you to use you as a vessel to help grow His Kingdom. He called you by name. Answer His call. Don't be afraid of anything because the Lord is your Protector. There is nothing stronger than the Lord. He has His hand on you. Don't run away from all the Lord is calling you to do. He won't leave you to do it all on your own. The Lord is your Helper. He will provide everything you need to accomplish your mission. Everything you need is within you. Don't look to the outside for help, but look deep within you. God is holding your hand as He builds you up.

You Can't Hide From God

"Where can I go from Your Spirit? Or where can I flee from Your presence? If I ascend into Heaven, You are there; If I make my bed in hell, behold, You are there. If I take the wings of the morning, And dwell in the uttermost parts of the sea, Even there Your hand shall lead me, And Your right hand shall hold me." Psalm 139:7-10 (NKJV)

When God calls out to you, there is nowhere you can run to get away from Him. You can't run from your calling forever. If God wants to use you, He will use you. When you run from God's calling on your life, things may get more difficult. The process becomes longer and more complicated as you run away. Surrender to the Lord and ask Him what it is He wants you to do. Stop running away. God will not leave you or abandon you. He will lead you on through His Holy Spirit as He holds you in His right hand.

FEBRUARY 28TH

God Will Fight For You

"And he shall say to them, 'Hear, O Israel: Today you are on the verge of battle with your enemies. Do not let your heart faint, do not be afraid, and do not tremble or be terrified because of them; for the Lord your God is He who goes with you, to fight for you against your enemies, to save you.'"
Deuteronomy 20:3-4 (NKJV)

The closer you are to your destination, the more your enemies will rise up against you. Satan will put obstacles in your path as you get closer to the promise, but don't be deceived. Satan is powerless. God has all power. Satan will use trickery to deceive you or to distract you from what is ahead. Your enemies are being used by Satan to take your eyes of the Lord and His promise, but use the power God has given you to defeat your enemies. God's Word is very powerful and effective. When you speak to a thing, it will have to move out of your way. When your enemies rise against you, God will defend you and all that came up against you will have to fall.

The Fullness Of God

———◆◇◆———

"I pray that out of His glorious riches He may strengthen you with power through His Spirit in your inner being, so that Christ may dwell in your hearts through faith. And I pray that you, being rooted and established in love, may have power, together with all the Lord's holy people, to grasp how wide and long and high and deep is the love of Christ, and to know this love that surpasses knowledge—that you may be filled to the measure of all the fullness of God." Ephesians 3:16-19 (NIV).

When you give your life to Christ, He strengthens your core. Christ is renewing you as He fills you with His love and power through the Holy Spirit. Now that you are rooted and established in His love, Christ is filling you with His power, along with His people, to work together for a greater cause. Allow the Lord to use you as a vessel to bring others into His love and into His Kingdom.

MARCH 2ND

My Heart Shall Not Fear

"Though an army may encamp against me, My heart shall not fear; Though war may rise against me, In this I will be confident." Psalm 27:3 (NKJV)

The enemy will send an attack against you to stop you from doing the Lord's work. He will do anything to discourage you or to make you feel afraid, but do not fear anything. You are being led by God's Spirit. He is protecting you under His wings. When your flesh dies, your spirit will live eternally with the Lord. There is no reason to fear your enemies. Your enemies can kill your body, but not your soul. God will bless your sacrifices for His Kingdom. Don't be afraid to speak the name of Jesus wherever the Lord leads you.

You Represent The Lord

——◆——

"Let us walk properly, as in the day, not in revelry and drunkenness, not in lewdness and lust, not in strife and envy."
Romans 13:13 (NKJV)

As a representative of Jesus Christ, it's important to carry yourself with class and dignity. Be careful of how you show yourself to others because it can affect the work that Christ wants to do through you. God sends you to certain places to use you as a vessel to minister to His people. He wants you to touch the hearts and lives of others, but if you aren't living clean, you may turn people away from the Lord. You are a representative for Jesus everywhere you go so practice self-control and allow the Lord to use you as a vessel to bring many souls into His Kingdom.

Your Heart Shall Rejoice Again

"And ye now therefore have sorrow: but I will see you again, and your heart shall rejoice, and your joy no man taketh from you." John 16:22 (KJV)

When you are going through a difficult time and you're feeling sorrowful, God will be with you through it all. He will not allow you to deal with hard times on your own. When God seems quiet in the midst of your trials, remember that He is still with you. The trials you experience in life are the best teachers. Your trials teach you how to use the power God put within you. It's important to learn how to use your pain as power. The painful parts of life are the very parts that will one day bless your life. Your struggles strengthen you for the purpose God gave you here on this earth. God will allow you to experience hard times and then set you free. God will turn around and use you to help bring others to freedom. When God brings you out of your suffering, He fills you with joy. No one on this earth will be able to steal your joy again.

Wait On The Lord

"Therefore the Lord will wait, that He may be gracious to you; And therefore He will be exalted, that He may have mercy on you. For the Lord is a God of justice; Blessed are all those who wait for Him." Isaiah 30:18 (NKJV)

It's exciting when the Lord moves you into new positions and higher levels, but sometimes the excitement of it all can cause you to go too fast. It can be frustrating when the Lord isn't moving fast enough, but God knows all things. He knows exactly when to bless you. When God doesn't move right away, it doesn't mean God is telling you no. He may just be telling you to wait. If God gave you everything you wanted as soon as you prayed for it, the thing you prayed for may overwhelm you if you're not fully prepared for the blessing. Wait on the Lord and allow Him to move you in His perfect timing. You will be blessed abundantly for your patience.

MARCH 6ᵀᴴ

Choose Your Friends Wisely

━━◈━━

"Make no friendship with an angry man, And with a furious man do not go, Lest you learn his ways And set a snare for your soul." Proverbs 22:24-25 (NKJV)

Be careful of who you associate with. It's not hard to become influenced by someone when you're always around that person. The enemy is really smooth. He knows exactly when to bring someone into your life that isn't good for you. This person can make you stumble and lose all you were working toward before they entered your life. There is nothing wrong with being respectful to everyone you cross paths with, but do not grow close to a person who loses their temper and is angry all the time. You will start to pick up some of their ways without even realizing it. You may lose good opportunities God is trying to bless you with if you allow yourself to fall into bad habits. The person you thought was a good friend may even turn his or her anger on you if you're not careful. Choose your friends wisely!

The Lord Is A Strong Tower

⬥

"The name of the Lord is a strong tower: the righteous runneth into it, and is safe." Proverbs 18:10 (KJV)

When you choose to give your life to Jesus Christ, He will keep you safe from the enemy. He will protect you when everything around you feels like it's falling apart and when you feel like the enemy is rising against you. You are covered under the blood of Jesus and everything under the blood is safe from harm. Remain in Christ as His Word teaches you and He will continue to hide you under His wing. Nothing can destroy you when you remain in God's hand.

God Provides All Things

———◆———

"And God is able to make all grace abound toward you, that you, always having all sufficiency in all things, may have an abundance for every good work." 2 Corinthians 9:8 (NKJV)

God is calling you to different places to accomplish His purpose. As you follow the Lord's direction, He will lead you to accomplish certain tasks for His Kingdom. Do not worry about what you will eat or what you will wear. God is your Provider. He will make sure you lack nothing as you work for Him. God pours out His grace over the righteous. He will never leave you to walk this journey alone. Continue to follow God's direction and He will bless you abundantly in His perfect timing.

God Uses Evil For His Good

⟫◆⟪

"But as for you, you meant evil against me; but God meant it for good, in order to bring it about as it is this day, to save many people alive." Genesis 50:20 (NKJV)

As you live your life here on this earth, the enemy will use whatever he can to destroy you because of the gifts God put within you. The enemy doesn't want you to discover the power which lies within you so he tries to find ways to hurt you. Everything the enemy uses against you, God will turn it around and make it work for your good. Just when you thought it was over and you couldn't go on any longer, God scooped you up in His hand. He cleansed you of impurities and now He is opening doors for you that no man can close. God is using you to help bring others into His light. He uses the least likely to do great works so no man can boast. He chose to purify you and exalt you to show Himself mighty through your transformation. When people look at how much your life has changed, there is no denying that Jesus is real.

MARCH 10ᵀᴴ

God Chooses Who He Will

―――◆―――

"As it is written, Jacob have I loved, but Esau have I hated. What shall we say then? Is there unrighteousness with God? God forbid. For He saith to Moses, I will have mercy on whom I will have mercy, and I will have compassion on whom I will have compassion." Romans 9:13-15 (KJV)

God chooses who He will. No one can tell God who to love and who to hate. No one can tell God who to bless and who not to bless. There may be people around you that are getting blessed, but you don't feel like they deserve it or have worked as hard as you. God is God. No one can tell Him to have mercy and compassion on this person, but not on that person. It's none of your business who God chooses to have compassion on. You just keep your eyes focused on what God told you to do. You can't walk someone else's path for them so mind your business and focus on what's happening on your path. You can't walk your own path when your eyes are on someone else's path. Follow the path God gave you to walk.

Envy Leads To Evil

"For where envy and self-seeking exist, confusion and every evil thing are there." James 3:16 (NKJV)

God chose to raise you up at a specific time for a special purpose. He made you with uniqueness. There is no one in the world like you. There is no reason to be jealous of anyone else. They have qualities that you don't, but you also have specific qualities that they don't have. You don't have to make yourself a star in everyone's eyes. God will do that for you. Keep your eyes on the prize, but most importantly on God. When you try to make yourself look good in the eyes of others, you lose what your mission was in the first place. Be great at what you do and you won't have to pretend to be great. God will bless your hard work and sacrifices. He will lift you up in His perfect timing if you remain humble. Ask God to remove anything that isn't of Him from you.

MARCH 12TH

Trust The Lord's Guidance

—◆—

"The Lord will guide you continually, And satisfy your soul in drought, And strengthen your bones; You shall be like a watered garden, And like a spring of water, whose waters do not fail." Isaiah 58:11 (NKJV)

Trust the Lord always. He will lead you wherever He needs you to go. Don't get discouraged when times get a little difficult. God will not allow you to go without anything. He will take care of you and bring you through whatever situation He brings you to. God is strengthening you through your struggles and He is teaching you how to be content in whatever situation you're put into. Trust the Lord's process fully and be patient. This too shall pass. God will bless you abundantly if you wait for Him.

The Lord's Goodness Will Follow

—◆—

"You prepare a table before me in the presence of my enemies; You anoint my head with oil; My cup runs over. Surely goodness and mercy shall follow me all the days of my life; And I will dwell in the house of the Lord forever." Psalm 23:5-6 (NKJV)

God anointed you and appointed you for something special, which means no man can stop God from moving you into your place of position. God put gifts within you that will bring you in front of great people. God will bless you in the face of your enemies and He will not allow not one of them to touch you as you remain in Him. God is lifting you into higher levels, but remember with more blessing comes more persecution. Stay focused on God's plan and keep your feet on His path. Do not allow yourself to stray from the path. God's grace and mercy are with you. His goodness goes with you wherever you go.

God Refined You

———◆———

"See, I have refined you, though not as silver; I have tested you in the furnace of affliction." Isaiah 48:10 (NIV)

Being a child of God won't always be easy. When God is moving you into another dimension in your life, He will allow you to go through the fire to refine you. God puts all His children through the fire in order to burn away all the impurities. He removes anything that will not work for you anymore as He moves you into the next phase of your life. Be joyful whenever you are going through trials because the trials are a sign that God is getting you ready for a new thing in your life. You are being pruned for the next level. He is cleaning you up to use you for His glory.

MARCH 15ᵀᴴ

Fear Nothing

"The Lord is my light and my salvation; whom shall I fear? The Lord is the strength of my life; of whom shall I be afraid?"
Psalm 27:1 (KJV)

The Lord has brought you into His light. He has saved you from eternal darkness. You are serving an all powerful God which means there is nothing or no one to fear. God's power lives within you so go after your purpose with confidence and boldness without any fear. God is your protector and He won't allow any harm to come near you. Do not be afraid to face any battle because God is holding you tightly in His mighty hand. If He calls you, trust that He will take care of you and all you need. God won't call you out of the dark into His light just to abandon you. He has called you to Him and now is your time to answer His call!

Rejoice, Pray, Give Thanks

—◆◆◆—

"Rejoice always, pray continually, give thanks in all circumstances; for this is God's will for you in Christ Jesus."
1 Thessalonians 5:16-18 (NIV)

Having an attitude of gratitude no matter what your circumstances are is so important. Being able to have joy during the more difficult times will allow you to become stronger and ready for anything that life may bring. Change your perspective on life by being content in every situation. Pray for understanding and ask God to show you what it is He wants you to learn or to change in your life. Always remember that after you win a battle you will receive a blessing. Pray for God's will to be done and not your own will. God's way can be difficult at times, but His way will make you a great warrior. Fight the good fight!

Value Others Above Yourself

—◈—

"Do nothing out of selfish ambition or vain conceit. Rather, in humility value others above yourselves, not looking to your own interests but each of you to the interests of the others."
Phillipians 2:3-4 (NIV)

God wants to use you as a vessel to help others, but when you are helping someone else, be sure to do it out of a pure heart. Do not help others to brag about it or to show off in front of others whenever you think they are watching. God knows your heart and He sees everything you do. Remain humble and help other people out of love. Do not exalt yourself above others. Value anyone that God blesses you with to help because He will reward you greatly for your sacrifices. Be ready to lift up others above yourself and God will lift you up.

Close Friends

———⊰✦⊱———

"A man that hath friends must shew himself friendly: and there is a friend that sticketh closer than a brother." Proverbs 18:24 (KJV)

Choose your friends wisely. Be careful who you allow to get close to you. Make sure that the friends you choose are reliable and trustworthy. People may let you down at times, but Jesus will never let you down. He will always be there to love you and to comfort you. Whenever you are feeling alone, turn to God first. He will be with you through all things, through the good times and the harder times. The process of coming into your calling can be overwhelming, but remember that Jesus is helping you through it all.

MARCH 19ᵀᴴ

Humility and Patience

———◇———

"With all lowliness and meekness, with longsuffering, forebearing one another in love; Endeavouring to keep the unity of the Spirit in the bond of peace." Ephesians 4:2 (KJV)

When God begins to take you higher in life, be careful not to allow pride to take over. Always remain humble and remember that it was God who lifted you higher in the first place. God decided to move you higher, but He can also decide to move you back down in order to keep you humble. When interacting with those around you, remain calm and gentle. When you are patient with others and not judgemental, it's easier for you to love them as God commands us to do. Loving others no matter what, allows you to build trust. No one is perfect and we are all still trying to find our way. Instead of judging others, help them along by loving them unconditionally.

MARCH 20TH

Walking in the Truth

———❖———

"I have no greater joy than to hear My children walk in truth."
3 John 1:4 (KJV)

As a child of God, you have the opportunity to show your gratitude to Him by walking in His light. God has done more in your life than you realize. Even the harder times are used to take away everything that won't benefit you as you come into your calling. You actually bring God joy when you walk in His truth. It's important to learn God's Word to understand what God's truth is. If you set aside some time to spend with God, it will be harder for the devil to deceive you. Walking in God's light allows you to see the world from His eyes and it changes the way you move. The more you obey God, the more power He fills you with to fulfill His purpose. Learn God's truth!

Be Content

———⬥———

"Nevertheless, each person should live as a believer in whatever situation the Lord has assigned to them, just as God has called them. This is the rule I lay down in all the churches."
1 Corinthians 7:17 (NIV)

When God calls you to a place, don't wish you were somewhere else. Be content in every situation knowing that God has brought you to that place for a reason. Ask God what it is that He wants you to do in that place. God does everything on purpose. If you are His, He will bring you into situations that are uncomfortable. This is how God grows you as a person. Every experience you go through is designed to take away things that aren't good for you or to add things to you. Get all that God wants you to have in the place you are in right now living as a believer.

Anger Can Lead to Evil

———◆———

"Refrain from anger and turn from wrath; do not fret—it leads only to evil. For those who are evil will be destroyed, but those who hope in the Lord will inherit the land." Psalm 37:8-9 (NIV)

There are going to be times when people or certain situations upset you. It's ok to be upset, but express the way you feel in a healthy way. Don't allow your anger to consume you. Anger eats away at you from the inside out. It leads you to do evil things. God doesn't reward this kind of behavior. He punishes this kind of behavior. God rewards those who hope in Him and those who turn to Him in times of trouble. God rewards peacemakers. If someone does something to hurt you, allow God to protect you. He will take care of your enemies. He will not let any harm come to His children.

Have Mercy On Me Lord

"Have mercy on me, my God, have mercy on me, for in You I take refuge. I will take refuge in the shadow of Your wings until the disaster has passed." Psalm 57:1 (NIV)

Whenever you are feeling afraid and don't know what will happen next in your life, remember that God will meet you in your scary place. God is with you in the dark place and He is waiting for you to reach out to Him. He is hiding you underneath His wings, protecting you from any evil that may rise up against you. No one is perfect and we all make mistakes as human beings. But God....... is very merciful and He forgives you for every single sin you've committed. He is Your protection and He is working all things out for your good. Thank Him and praise Him continuously. This is how you gain access to God.

Don't Be Surprised By Trials

---◆---

"Dear friends, do not be surprised at the fiery ordeal that has come on you to test you, as though something strange were happening to you." 1 Peter 4:12 (NIV)

Whenever God is bringing you into another level in your life, you have to go through the fire first. When it feels like darkness is breaking loose in your life, stand strong in the Lord knowing that He is only testing you to strengthen you for the next new thing. When trouble is coming at you from every side, don't get discouraged. God is taking you higher. When God gives you more, Satan also attacks you more. When you make it through this trial, you will come into a higher position in your life. Get ready for your next level and blessing!

Return to the Lord

"Come, let us return to the Lord. He has torn us to pieces, but He will heal us; He has injured us but, He will bind up our wounds. After two days He will revive us; on the third day He will restore us, that we may live in His presence." Hosea 6:1-2 (NIV)

As human beings, we are born into sin. We like to do things our own way, not thinking about the consequences of our actions. After life has torn us down, God will come in to heal us and to put us back together again. If you are hurting or feeling torn apart, it's time to make a choice. Do you want to continue down the road to destruction or will you allow the Lord to revive you and restore you. He will not make you choose Him. He blesses us with freewill. Do you want to die in darkness or live freely in God's light?

God Blesses Your Faithfulness

"His master replied, 'Well done, good and faithful servant! You have been faithful with a few things; I will put you in charge of many things. Come and share your master's happiness!'" Matthew 25:23 (NIV)

God will give you things that He wants you to do. Before God will bless you with more, He wants to see that you will be faithful with what He has already given you to do. God is strengthening you and growing you through every level He brings you into. God will not move you into the next thing if you can't be trusted with the first things He has given you. When God sees your faithfulness on this level, He will give you more on the next level. God wants to give you excess and abundance in your life. Show Him you can be trusted with more and He will give you more.

Reap Your Harvest

―――◆◆◆――――

"And let us not be weary in well doing: for in due season we shall reap, if we faint not." Galatians 6:9 (KJV)

Following Jesus isn't going to feel great all the time. You will come into situations that make you feel unsure of yourself. As you move into a new dimension of your life, everything you thought you knew starts to change. When God moves you into something new, it makes you feel uncertain about the future. This feeling isn't a bad thing. You're growing and when God grows you, it hurts a little. Keep trusting Him in the scary places and continue doing what He is asking you to do. As you follow His instruction, things will come together in His time. No matter how much it hurts, don't give up. He will bless you greatly if you don't quit!

MARCH 28TH

Crushed in Spirit

———=◆=———

"The Lord is close to the brokenhearted and saves those who are crushed in spirit." Psalm 34:18 (NIV)

God will allow you to be crushed so that you learn to depend on Him in everything. There are blessings in the breaking of your heart. When your spirit is crushed and your heart is broken, you are given the opportunity to lean on God more than ever through these difficult times. He wants you to get to know Him more intimately. God will not allow you to suffer the crushing alone. He will walk through this darkness with you. Do not fear your enemies because God goes ahead of you and defeats them all. Stay close to Him through this time and thank Him constantly for being the light you need to find your way out.

MARCH 29TH

God Has You Surrounded

———◆———

"As the mountains surround Jerusalem, so the Lord surrounds His people both now and forevermore." Psalm 125:2 (NIV)

God has you on a great journey Home. Walking with the Lord is such a beautiful experience, but also challenging at times. As you go where He calls you to go, there will be enemies waiting to take you down that want to keep you from reaching your destination. There will be huge mountains to climb. Satan has assigned demons to keep you from making it to your destination, but God has all of your enemies surrounded as they surround you. Keep walking while having faith in the Lord to do what He promised you. Don't allow your feelings to trump what you know. You may feel bad in the midst of trials, but you know that God is with you and He will give you the victory!

Care For Your Own

— ⟫◆⟪ —

"But if any provide not for his own, and specially for those of his own house, he hath denied the faith, and is worse than an infidel." 1 Timothy 5:8 (KJV)

Be grateful for the family God has blessed you with. There are some people who don't have any family to help them through the journey of life. If God blesses you with family and He provides for your every need, you should also help provide for your family if it is in your power to do so. God blesses you so that you can bless others. Your blessing is not only for you, but also for those God brings into your life to bless. God blesses those He can trust to help others when they are down and out. God gave you abundance, but He can also take it away. Be sure to help whoever God gives you to help.

Feed Your Enemies

"Therefore 'If your enemy is hungry, feed him; If he is thirsty, give him a drink; For in so doing you will heap coals of fire on his head.' Do not be overcome by evil, but overcome evil with good." Romans 12:20-21 (NIV)

Everyone has enemies at some point in life. Your enemies usually rise up when something huge is happening in your life. People become your enemy when they see you doing great things and jealousy rises up within them. If your enemies come up against you, don't respond in anger. Anger opens up the door to evil. When you allow anger to rise up, you put yourself in a dangerous place. You lose your peace. If someone does evil against you, do good to them. There is power in doing good to your enemies. God remains in control of how the story plays out in the end.

A New Heart and Spirit

"Rid yourselves of all the offenses you have committed, and get a new heart and a new spirit. Why will you die, people of Israel? For I take no pleasure in the death of anyone, declares the Sovereign Lord. Repent and live!" Ezekiel 18:31-32 (NIV)

We are all born sinners. The wage for sin is death. We would all die for our sins, but Jesus died in our place. God doesn't want us to die, but He gives us the choice to choose life or death. God chose you to cleanse you and to make you new. When God calls you, He gives you free will. You can choose Him or this world. If you choose God, He puts you through a series of tests. He refines you as gold by putting you through the fire. Repent daily, remain strong, while continuing to live freely in Christ.

Contentment

———◆———

"Not that I speak in respect of want: for I have learned, in whatsoever state I am, therewith to be content." Philippians 4:11 (KJV)

There are ups and downs as you go through life. Some days you feel on top of the world and have more than enough. Other days you sit and wonder where your next meal is coming from. But God, He is a good God and He won't allow His children to go without. He provides all you need when you need it. You need the difficult times to learn how to trust God in every circumstance. God will always show up for His children. Remember to help others when they're having a hard time because you never know when you will need help yourself. When others can see the sacrifice you have made to help others, they are quicker to help you when you are down.

Trust God's Path

"Trust in the Lord with all your heart and lean not on your own understanding; in all your ways submit to Him, and He will make your paths straight." Proverbs 3:5-6 (NIV)

Whenever you're going through trials, it's easy to fall into self-pity. You start feeling like you're the only person going through hard times, but it's not true. Everyone God chooses has to go through the fire first to remove anything that is not of Him before He can use you. Although you may not understand why you are suffering certain things in the moment, praise God and thank Him for strengthening you through your trials. Trust God no matter how difficult things may feel right now, knowing that God is working all things out for your good. Give all you have to God and He will straighten your path.

APRIL 4TH

Forgive And Be Forgiven

—⫸⬦⫷—

*"For if you forgive other people when they sin against you,
your Heavenly Father will also forgive you. But if you do not
forgive others their sins, your Father will not forgive your sins."*
Matthew 6:14-15 (NIV)

People are going to hurt you at some point in your
life, including family and friends. Holding onto grudges
only hurts you in the end. Although forgiving others
who hurt you can be difficult, you have to forgive them
for your own peace of mind. You have to be the bigger
person and realize that giving someone a piece of your
mind will only take your peace of mind. Everyone
sins. If you want God to forgive you when you sin,
then you have to be willing to forgive others. Life is
difficult enough as it is. Stop holding onto unnecessary
pain and move on.

Remaining Humble

—◆—

*"Rejoice greatly, Daughter Zion Shout, Daughter Jerusalem!
See, your King comes to you, righteous and victorious, lowly
and riding on a donkey, on a colt, the foal of a donkey."
Zechariah 9:9 (NIV)*

Jesus is our King and He is worthy to be praised. Although Jesus is a King, He remained very humble. He chose to ride on a donkey while being the King of all things. We too must remain humble. If you are filled with humility, God will lift you up in His perfect timing. As a child of the Most High, you are also righteous and victorious, but allow God to exalt you. If you place yourself above everything and everyone, God will humble you. It doesn't feel very good when God decides to humble you. Continue walking with God and He will make you victorious.

Open Doors

"For everyone that asketh receiveth; and he that seeketh findeth; and to him that knocketh it shall be opened." Luke 11:10 (KJV)

We have a great God who loves to bless His children. God loves it when His children reach out for Him. He reveals Himself to all who asks to see Him. God won't turn you away. You will find Him if you search for Him. Your whole perspective on life changes when God opens the door for you to enter. There will be trials to face, but the Holy Spirit will train you and God will protect you. Make sure you are prepared for any attack the enemy sends against you. Once God opens the door, the attacks will become greater. Satan doesn't want you to find your true purpose. Knock on God's door and He will open it, but be ready to fight the good fight.

New Every Morning

———≼⬥≽———

"Because of the Lord's great love we are not consumed, for His compassions never fail. They are new every morning; great is Your faithfulness." Lamentations 3:22-23 (NIV)

God is a very compassionate, understanding, and forgiving God. Our Heavenly Father already knew that none of us were going to live this life perfectly without making mistakes, so He gave us His Son, Jesus. If you fail, it's ok to get back up and try it again. People may judge you, but God forgives you for all sin. There isn't one perfect person walking this earth. Every morning is a new chance to start all over again and to do things better than you did them yesterday. Thank God every morning for His great compassion and learn from your mistakes by doing things better than you did them the day before.

Heavenly Gifts From God

"Every good gift and every perfect gift is from above, and cometh down from the Father of lights, with whom is no variableness, neither shadow of turning." James 1:17 (KJV)

God chose you from the beginning. He created you to do wonderful things for His Kingdom. His gifts come from Heaven and they are perfect. The only person who can destroy that gift is you. Anything God gives you remains within you no matter how hard the enemy fights you. God put you on this earth to do amazing things. Ask Him what He put you on this earth to change. Thank Him for His guidance daily and for His grace as you chase after your calling. God wants you to choose His path. He will show you things you've thought you'd never see. Buckle up and prepare for the ride God wants to take you on.

God Is In Control

"I have seen something else under the sun: The race is not to the swift or the battle to the strong, nor does food come to the wise or wealth to the brilliant or favor to the learned; but time and chance happen to them all." Ecclesiastes 9:11 (NIV)

There are going to be different seasons in your life. One minute you will feel on top of the world and then the next minute you are wondering if you will make it through the next few months ahead. At the end of the day, God is in control of everything. If this season of your life isn't going the way you'd hoped it would go, continue trusting Him in the process. Remain in Him and He will keep you. We need all seasons to grow. It may be storming in your life right now, but the sun will come out again. This too shall pass.

God Anointed You

—⬦—

"As for you, the anointing you received from Him remains in you, and you do not need anyone to teach you. But as His anointing teaches you about all things and as that anointing is real, not counterfeit—just as it has taught you, remain in Him." 1 John 2:27 (NIV)

When God anoints you to do something mighty in His Kingdom, don't be surprised by the attack that comes upon you. The devil knew how mighty and gifted you would be in God's Kingdom. That's why you are experiencing an attack in your life. Satan has assigned certain demons to distract you from your purpose. Remain under God's wing and He will protect you in this time. Resist Satan and he will flee. You are being attacked because of the powerful gift God put within you, but God is keeping you covered.

APRIL 11TH

Rejection

"He was despised and rejected by mankind, a man of suffering, and familiar with pain. Like one from whom people hide their faces He was despised, and we held Him in low esteem." Isaiah 53:3 (NIV)

Everyone is hurting in some area of their life. People may act out in ways others don't understand. God is using the rejection of others for your good. If you have ever been rejected, praise God in your suffering. Not everyone is good for you as God moves you closer to your promise. God is removing certain people away from you so that He can continue transforming you into the person He has called you to be. Thank God for rejection because He has set you apart to do amazing things. You were not meant to fit in with everyone else.

Peace Gives You Life

———⬥———

"A sound heart is life to the body, But envy is rottenness to the bones." Proverbs 14:30 (NKJV)

Be very careful not to fall into the trap of jealousy. Don't allow yourself to dwell on the things you feel like God has never given you or to compare your blessings with that of another. Count the many blessings God has given you. As you walk in gratitude for all the gifts you've received from God, your gratitude activates God to bless you with more. Be happy for the blessings that others receive and God will begin to shower you with blessings as well. Being envious of others will only kill your spirit, but remaining in peace at all times will give you more life. When you see others get blessed, be grateful for them knowing that your blessings will soon come.

Escaping Corruption

—⟨⟩◆⟨⟩—

"Through these He has given us His very great and precious promises, so that through them you may participate in the divine nature, having escaped the corruption in the world caused by evil desires." 2 Peter 1:4 (NIV)

God gives all of His children great promises, but you won't receive His promises without going through the process. Everything that becomes anything great goes through a great process first. Process doesn't feel good, but it is necessary to strengthen you for the promise God has for you. Process removes all things that corrupt the person God created you to be. You can't remain the same and expect great blessings to rain down in your life. God is cleansing you through your suffering. You will come into your great promise after you come through this process. Thank Him for the person He is growing you into today.

Not Destroyed

—✦—

"We are hard pressed on every side, but not crushed; perplexed, but not in despair; persecuted, but not abandoned; struck down, but not destroyed." 2 Corinthians 4:8-9 (NIV)

Storms will break out in your life causing you to question God. You feel like you're the only person going through dark times, but it's simply not true. God isn't trying to destroy you. He is using the storms to strengthen you for what He promised you. God can't use you if you insist on being the same person forever. Be willing to learn from your past. Stop blaming others. You may be hurting right now, but keep thanking Him for the person He is molding you to be through this pressing in your life. He is shaping you and it hurts, but this pain won't compare to the glory that will be revealed within you.

Do You Want Better?

"When Jesus saw him lying there, and knew that he had already been in that condition a long time, He said to him, 'Do you want to be made well?'" John 5:6 (NKJV)

You may be going through times that feel paralyzing to you right now. You feel stuck in the same place you've always been. It's hard to even get out of the bed on certain days. Life is going to be difficult at times, but everyone will experience these moments at some point in their lives. God's question to you is, "Do you want to get well?" He's giving you the choice to stay lying down while everyone else is getting up. They're running after their blessings, dreams, and promises. God won't make you get better, but He's right here waiting for you to reach out to Him. Do you want what He has for you, yes or no? You choose!

Gratitude Activates More

―――⋙◆⋘―――

"Taking the five loaves and the two fish and looking up to Heaven, He gave thanks and broke the loaves. Then He gave them to His disciples to distribute to the people. He also divided the two fish among them all." Mark 6:41 (NIV)

There are times in your life you wonder how you're going to make it through, but Jesus gives us an example of how God stretches what you have. Jesus fed a whole multitude of people with 5 loaves of bread and 2 fish. He taught us to be grateful for everything God gives you. Trust God to provide all that you need and more. God will bless you more abundantly when you have faith in Him and can thank Him even in the times you only have a little. Allow God to see your gratitude in all circumstances and He will rain down His blessings over you.

Resurrection

---◆---

"For if we have been united together in the likeness of His death, certainly we also shall be in the likeness of His resurrection, knowing this, that our old man was crucified with Him, that the body of sin might be done away with, that we should no longer be slaves of sin." Romans 6:5-6 (NKJV)

Jesus went through some very horrible, painful things on the cross. He sacrificed His life so you could be free. If you choose to give Him your life, you need to understand that you will suffer at times for Him. God will honor your sacrifice. He is making you victorious. If you can make it through this painful time, God will pour out His favor and His blessings over you as you walk with Him. You are being made whole at this very moment. God is strengthening you through this process. You can't quit. Keep moving forward, pressing toward the mark. God will bless you for your obedience as you remain close to Him in the storm.

APRIL 18ᵀᴴ

Jesus Lives On

———◆———

"God has raised this Jesus to life, and we are all witnesses of it. Exalted to the right hand of God, He has received from the Father the promised Holy Spirit and has poured out what you now see and hear." Acts 2:32-33 (NIV)

After Jesus died on the cross, He came to His disciples and showed Himself strong. They knew He was the true Son of God. He is now sitting at the right hand of God. You have the power of the Holy Spirit because of what Jesus did for you. The Holy Spirit will teach you all you need to know. He will mold you and lead you wherever He wants you to go to do God's work. Trust God and His guidance no matter how scary things may look or feel. Before you start your day, ask God to show you the way. He won't forsake you. Trust Him in all your endeavors.

You Are More Than a Conquer

―――◆―――

"And those He predestined, He also called; those He called, He also justified; those He justified, He also glorified. What, then, shall we say in response to these things? If God is for us, who can be against us?" Romans 8:30-31 (NIV)

God chose you from the beginning of the world for something great. You'll know when God calls you. When God calls you, things you used to do won't feel right anymore. You start to actually want to change for the better. God will transform you, making you righteous. After your transformation, God will fill you with His royal power, making you beautiful. No one can stop you from reaching your destiny. When God calls you to greatness, anyone who rises up against you will fall. Run after your purpose without stopping and receive God's promise.

Genuine Love

⟨—⬥—⟩

"Love bears all things, believes all things, hopes all things, endures all things." 1 Corinthians 13:7 (ESV)

Love can be a very stressful thing, but it's worth it. Although Jesus suffered painfully, He did it for you. Every blow He took was for you. The many stripes across His back was so that you could be healed from your infirmities. His suffering allowed you to be free. Imitate the love of Christ in your love for others. When the people you love and trust hurt you deeply, continue to love them through it. If you truly love someone, you will be right there for them to the end even when there is no advantage in loving them. Continue loving that person through their time of suffering because real love, true love will transform the hardest person.

Encourage Others

—◆—

"And let us consider how we may spur one another on toward love and good deeds, not giving up meeting together, as some are in the habit of doing, but encouraging one another—and all the more as you see the Day approaching." Hebrews 10:24-25 (NIV)

God brings people into your life for a reason. Make sure you're doing whatever it is God is asking you to do with that person. Encourage them to do great things and love them unconditionally. Don't give up so easily on them because you could be the one God is using to save their life and bring them into His Kingdom. Everything won't always go the way you expect it to go. It may not be a smooth transition, but forgive them like God forgives you. No one knows the exact hour Jesus is coming back so make every moment with that person count.

Forgiveness Leads to Love

⟸⟹⟸

"Therefore, I tell you, her many sins have been forgiven—as her great love has shown. But whoever has been forgiven little loves little." Luke 7:47 (NIV)

When God forgives you, it's the best feeling in the world. You are filled with great love, perfect peace, and joy. His love erases all the bad that has happened in your past and He continues to pour out His grace over you as you follow Him. You can usually spot one of God's children by the way they love others. God's children who love the greatest are the ones who have been forgiven the most. God's love cleans up your past. He fills you with His Holy Spirit allowing you to be a leader for others to follow. Thank God daily for sacrificing His only Son so that you could live freely in this life and for eternity.

Control Your Tongue

"Sin is not ended by multiplying words, but the prudent hold their tongues." Proverbs 10:19 (NIV)

When dealing with others, it's not easy to be quiet when you have a disagreement with them. Everyone wants to justify their side and the reason they are right. If someone is talking the whole time and won't let you get a word in, it doesn't mean they're right. The wisest thing to do when the person is talking continuously is hold your tongue. Eventually the person will stop and maybe then you could discuss things later when everything has cooled down. When you're right about something, you don't have to prove yourself. The truth always prevails. Don't get frustrated by the person's many words, just remain calm and in peace. Use wisdom by allowing God to fight your battle.

God is in Control, Be Still

"Be still, and know that I am God; I will be exalted among the nations, I will be exalted in the earth." Psalm 46:10 (NKJV)

As you continue following Christ and getting closer to your destination, Satan will send a demonic attack against you. Satan tries to keep you from becoming the powerful child of God that you were created to be. The higher up you get, the stronger the attack will be on your life. Don't get discouraged by any attack the enemy sends. Instead, praise God and thank Him because you know that attacks become stronger as you get closer to God's promise. When painful attacks come upon you, don't try to resist what is happening by hiding away in the darkness. Remain in perfect peace by being still and remembering that God has already won the battle.

APRIL 25TH

Walk in God's Path

———◈———

"This is what the Lord says: 'Stand at the crossroads and look; ask for the ancient paths, ask where the good way is, and walk in it, and you will find rest for your souls. But you said, 'We will not walk in it.'" Jeremiah 6:16 (NIV)

After life breaks you, God gives you two choices. You can choose to live the same way you always have or you can choose to walk with God. If you choose God's path, He will give you rest from the many burdens you carry daily. God is calling out to you because He wants to give you the desires of your heart. He loves to bless His children. He pours His favor out over His children as they follow Him. Which way will you choose today? Do you want to live in perfect peace and freedom or do you want to continue walking in darkness?

Your Rod and Staff Comfort Me

"Even though I walk through the darkest valley, I will fear no evil, for You are with me, Your rod and Your staff, they comfort me." Psalm 23:4 (NIV)

When you're walking through a dark valley and you're hurting, lift your eyes to the sky remembering God is with you as you walk toward the mountain. All kinds of troubles may come as you run after your dream, but God will bless your tenacity. God knows your sacrifice and He will pour out His favor over you as you fight for your purpose. Once you reach the peak of the mountain, be sure to bow down and thank Him for bringing you to the top. Never forget who brought you into the place you're in now. Your gratitude and humility will unlock many more doors. God will bless whatever your hands touch and wherever your feet walk.

God's Word is Our Daily Bread

"He humbled you, causing you to hunger and then feeding you with manna, which neither you nor your ancestors had known, to teach you that man does not live on bread alone but on every word that comes from the mouth of the Lord."
Deuteronomy 8:3 (NIV)

It can be painful at first when God chooses you. God will take away everything you have to get your attention and to humble you. Anything you put before God will be taken away. He shows you how unimportant material things are if you don't have Him. Material things can't fill the void within you, only God can do that. He owns it all anyway so put Him first and He will give you the desires of your heart. Start your mornings with God everyday and watch how many blessings He rains down over you.

God Chooses The Weak

⬥

"But God chose the foolish things of the world to shame the wise; God chose the weak things of the world to shame the strong. God chose the lowly things of this world and the despised things—and the things that are not—to nullify the things that are, so that no one may boast before Him." 1 Corinthians 1:27-29 (NIV)

God shows Himself strongest in your weakness. After He transforms you, others will know how real and amazing God truly is by looking at who you used to be compared to who you are today. God chooses the least of us in the world and makes us mighty to glorify Himself. God broke you to keep you from falling into pride. Remember, it's because of Him you're closer to your destiny. Remain grateful, remain humble as He lifts you up and blesses you with success.

Restore Others Gently

"Brethren, if a man is overtaken in any trespass, you who are spiritual restore such a one in a spirit of gentleness, considering yourself lest you also be tempted." Galatians 6:1 (NKJV)

Everyone has some kind of fault. You have to remember this when you are helping someone who has been overtaken by their sins. Before you go to help that person, pray to the Lord for guidance through the Holy Spirit. Allow God to use you as a vessel to help the person who is lost in darkness. Be careful not to judge them since we all have sinned. Use humility and gentleness to help them get back on track. If you are gentle with them, they are more likely to hear you out. If you are not gentle and use anger, it will only push them further away from the light. Use love to correct them.

God Holds You Up

⇒•◇•⇐

"The Lord makes firm the steps of the one who delights in Him; though he may stumble, he will not fall, for the Lord upholds him with His hand." Psalm 37:23-24 (NIV)

God is a God of timing and His timing is perfect. There's a time and season for everything. As you run after your promise, God orders your steps. Some seasons won't feel as good as other seasons, but continue to trust God as He holds you in His hand. When God is taking you through a process, it won't feel so great and it will get difficult, but it won't compare to the glory that will be revealed within you when you reach the promise. God sticks to a certain schedule, but sometimes God will bless you out of nowhere. He will give you blessings that make no sense at all. Remain faithful, trusting Him always.

Seek The Good Of Others

—⬥—

"I have the right to do anything,' you say—but not everything is beneficial. 'I have the right to do anything'—but not everything is constructive. No one should seek their own good, but the good of others." 1 Corinthians 10:23-24 (NIV)

It's good to be strong and independent, but in Christ. Depend on God and rest in His power. You are given free will to choose your own path, but your way is not the best way. God's path can be challenging at times, but He strengthens you and is with you through every trial. God's path grows a great love and respect within you for the journey of others. After being humbled by God, you realize that you need Him. Life is meaningless without Him. God put you in your right place not just for you, but to reach out to the people around you.

Live in God's Safety

"For the waywardness of the simple will kill them, and the complacency of fools will destroy them; but whoever listens to Me will live in safety and be at ease, without fear of harm."
Proverbs 1:32-33 (NIV)

Be sure to ask the Lord for His guidance daily. Be careful not to run after your destiny in your own power. You're just a human being who will tire out eventually, but God is all powerful and He will sustain you for the promise He's given you. Find your purpose and go after it with your whole heart. Your purpose will keep you alive and well. It's hard to want to live if you have nothing to live for. Your dream and purpose will give you life. As you chase after your calling, God will lead you and He will open all the right doors for you. He will give you discernment about the next step to take, but be willing to listen to Him and to follow His guidance. God will keep you safe underneath His wings, protecting you from harm.

Skilled In Your Work

—◆—

"Do you see a man who excels in his work? He will stand before kings; he will not stand before unknown men." Proverbs 22:29 (NKJV)

God gave you gifts, but it's up to you to cultivate those gifts. As you grow your gifts, God will bring you in rooms that you've never dreamed of. God will use you in ways you could never imagine. God is a God of great creativity and if you are His child, you have inherited the gift of creativity. Although God gave you special gifts, it's your choice to use those gifts to glorify Him. God has instilled gifts within you and they will grow the most when you are put in uncomfortable situations. Your gifts were given to you in order to help change the world and the people around you. How does your gift meet the needs of others?

Guard Your Heart

"Keep your heart with all diligence, For out of it spring the issues of life." Proverbs 4:23 (NKJV)

Your heart is one of the most fragile things you have. You can't give your heart to just anybody. Everyone won't respect it. Be sure to ask for guidance when it comes to giving your heart away to someone. Listen to what God is telling you or you will end up broken-hearted. Your heart is to love God's people and to help bring others closer to God. Your heart is filled with passion for God's purpose, but it's hard to run after your passion with a broken heart. It can be done, but it makes it a lot harder when it's broken. Save your heart for the person God has for you. Respect yourself enough not to give your heart to someone who won't value it. Guard your heart with your life.

A Cheerful Heart

⊰⬧⊱

"A cheerful heart is good medicine, but a crushed spirit dries up the bones." Proverbs 17:22 (NIV)

Life can be very challenging, especially when you are moving into higher levels. Before you come into a new level, there will always be a battle to fight before God moves you into the next new thing in your life. It's important to have fun as you follow Christ into higher levels. Laughter is healing to your soul. Joy strengthens your spirit and prepares you for the next fight. Bitterness can make you sick and is very harmful to your body. Your body will eventually start to break down if you allow bitterness and anger to drive you. Relax a little and enjoy the journey Home. Allow yourself to laugh sometimes. What good is having everything if you never enjoy it?

God's Love Won't Leave You

⟞◆⟝

"I will be his Father, and he will be My son. When he does wrong, I will punish him with a rod wielded by men, with floggings inflicted by human hands. But My love will never be taken away from him, as I took it away from Saul, whom I removed from before you." 2 Samuel 7:14-15 (NIV)

God will go ahead of you and devour any enemies who lie in wait for you. He will move people out of certain positions to make you the head person in charge, but if you step out of line, He will correct you. God is your Father and He won't allow you to continue in sin without any consequences for your actions, but His favor will still be on you because of His love for you. Correct your wrongdoings. Don't allow distractions to take you out of the position God blessed you with. Stay focused.

Show Children The Way

———◆———

"Start children off on the way they should go, and even when they are old they will not turn from it." Proverbs 22:6 (NIV)

It's crucial to instill great values within your children such as love, kindness, respect, patience, forgiveness, and wisdom. The way you raise a child up has a lot to do with what they become in the future. Put them in environments that will help them grow. Teach them skills at an early age. Put them in places that will help to draw out their gifts and develop their gifts. Children learn by watching, which is why it's important to have them in good and safe environments. It's hard to unlearn values once they are instilled within you. It can be done, but it makes it more difficult for a child to relearn new values. Lead them toward a brighter future.

Delivered By God

⟫◆⟪

"He has delivered us from such a deadly peril, and He will deliver us again. On Him we have set our hope that He will continue to deliver us, as you help us by your prayers. Then many will give thanks on our behalf for gracious favor granted us in answer to the prayers of many." 2 Corinthians 1:10-11 (NIV)

There are many of us who fall into some kind of sin or trap from the devil. Satan is very smooth and he will attack you through things or people you never would've imagined. Sometimes he attacks your loved ones around you, which can be very painful to watch. It's important to pray for your family and friends. Put aside some time to pray for the people you love daily. Pray for all Christians around the world to be raised up, strengthened, and used for a time such as this. God has always delivered His children out of bondage and He will continue to deliver all who are His.

Seek God First

"But seek first His Kingdom and His righteousness, and all these things will be given to you as well." Matthew 6:33 (NIV)

Don't wait until you get blessed to seek God. Seek Him first every morning and God will bless you for it. Times will get hard and you may have to struggle. Even when you are struggling, be sure to seek God first in all you do and He will open up the windows of Heaven to bless you. God will allow hard times to come upon you to see if you are only seeking Him for things. Will you remain faithful to Him when you're not sure where your next meal is coming from? If God can trust you to serve Him in the famine, He will pour you out a blessing you won't have room enough to receive. Serve God in the famine and God will bless you abundantly in the promise.

God Will Not Leave You

—⟶◆⟵—

"Then Elijah said to him, 'Stay here; the Lord has sent me to the Jordan.' And he replied, 'As surely as the Lord lives and as you live, I will not leave you.' So the two of them walked on." 2 Kings 2:6 (NIV)

At the end of the day, all you have is your word. If you tell someone that you're going to be there with them until the end, do it. Obstacles will come as you walk with people you love, but loyalty means more than the obstacles that rise up to separate you. If you love someone and you're committed to them, there is nothing that can pull you away from that person. Work through your issues and grow stronger together to reach the goals ahead of you. Be grateful for the people who love you through your weaknesses. You are blessed to have loyal people in your life.

Press On Toward The Mark

"Brothers and sisters, I do not consider myself yet to have taken hold of it. But one thing I do: Forgetting what is behind and straining toward what is ahead, I press on toward the goal to win the prize for which God has called me Heavenward in Christ Jesus." Philippians 3:13-14 (NIV)

Everyone has a past. For many of us, the past is very painful. There were days in your past that felt unbearable. It felt like you'd never overcome certain obstacles, but you did. Some of the people around you didn't make it. There is a reason you're still here. God has something He wants you to do. Don't allow your past to hold you captive. Use your past experiences as building blocks instead of stumbling blocks. Build a powerful empire with the building blocks God blessed you with.

Fear God

———◆———

"For in the multitude of dreams and many words there are also divers vanities: but fear thou God." Ecclesiastes 5:7 (KJV)

Many of us have dreams about what we want to accomplish in this life. It's a great thing to dream big and to have dreams about touching the lives of others. Continue to dream of making a difference and of making your mark on this earth, but also realize dreams don't come true unless you do the work to accomplish your dreams. Sitting around dreaming won't get you anywhere. You have to physically make moves toward your dream. Set goals for yourself. The difference between dreams and goals are setting dates. When you set a date to make a move, it is no longer just a dream. Setting a date makes it now a goal. Continue to dream big dreams, but also set dates to achieve your goals.

Your Testimony Will Save Others

---◆---

"Her neighbors and relatives heard that the Lord had shown her great mercy, and they shared her joy." Luke 1:58 (NIV)

When God chose to bless you, it wasn't a secret. The people around you knew God was real after He transformed you. Your loved ones couldn't deny God's power after seeing you change. God poured out His mercy over you. When others saw how gracious God had been to you, it made it easier for them to come to Him. People who knew you before could see the power of God through your transformation. He's using you at this very moment to bring others closer to Him. Allow God to use you as a vessel to help save others from their darkness. Your loved ones are more likely to open their eyes once they see God's power in your life. You're blessed to be the chosen one.

Repent For Your Sins

"I tell you that in the same way there will be more rejoicing in Heaven over one sinner who repents than over ninety-nine righteous persons who do not need to repent." Luke 15:7 (NIV)

There are people who feel lost with nowhere to go. The further they fall into sin, the darker life feels to them. BUT GOD, will meet you in your darkest place. He will bring you into His light. He loves us all equally, but God and the Heavens rejoice more over one sinner coming to the light. God uses the sinner who has repented in mighty ways. He uses them to bring others out of their life of sin. If God will transform one sinner, why wouldn't He do it for another sinner? It doesn't matter how bad you think your sin is. A sin is a sin and God will still use you mightily in His Kingdom.

Two Cannot Easily Be Broken

———◇———

"And if one prevail against him, two shall withstand him; and a threefold cord is not quickly broken." Ecclesiastes 4:12 (KJV)

One of the most dangerous things you can do is isolate yourself from everyone. It's good to have alone time, but it's important to do things that help you grow as a person in that alone time. Don't isolate yourself all the time. You can't encourage who you won't talk to. Grow in your relationship with God and build you a great team of loyal people. Keep trustworthy people around you that will help you fight the good fight when the enemy rises up against you. It's easier for the enemy to defeat you by attacking your mind if you're always alone. Having God and a great team gives you a much better protection. Build your team using discernment.

Everyone Has Faults

⟫◆⟪

"For we all stumble in many things. If anyone does not stumble in word, he is a perfect man, able also to bridle the whole body." James 3:2 (NKJV)

Being a believer in Jesus doesn't mean you won't make mistakes. No one walking this earth is perfect. Jesus was the only perfect person to walk this earth. Don't allow someone's opinion to stop you from walking with God. You may sin in a moment of weakness, but any sins you commit are between you and God. The people who judge you have also sinned and will probably sin again. In the end, you're working to please God, not people. People who judge you don't realize that you're not the person you used to be, but you're working hard to be the person God has called you to be. Continue to grow in God as you run after your calling.

Do Not Destroy One Another

"But if ye bite and devour one another, take heed that ye be not consumed one of another." Galatians 5:15 (KJV)

God puts specific people in your life for a specific reason at a specific time. Nothing God does is an accident. He puts whoever He needs to put around you in order to help develop you. God strategically places your enemies around you. He uses your enemies to grow you and push you into the next level of life. When God places good people around you, be careful not to destroy them. You need others to accomplish a bigger goal. If you destroy the people God has given you to run with, you destroy your purpose. If you have a falling out with your brother, go and make it right. Do everything on your part to keep the peace. Strengthen one another. Make the dream a reality.

God's Spirit Will Lead You

———⟫•◇•⟪———

"Teach me to do thy will; for thou art my God: thy spirit is good; lead me into the land of uprightness." Psalm 143:10 (KJV)

As children of God, we are all trying to find our way to our real Home. This life here on earth is temporary. No one will be here forever. God placed you here on this earth to accomplish a certain purpose. Look to God for answers for who He created you to be and what He created you to do. Follow God's lead by asking the Holy Spirit for guidance before you start your day every morning and throughout the day. As you learn more about who God is, He will reveal more and more of your purpose to you. He has destined you for greatness. Once you find out what your calling is here on earth, you will be unstoppable. Keep searching for your true purpose.

God Gave You Authority

"He replied, 'I saw Satan fall like lightning from Heaven. I have given you authority to trample on snakes and scorpions and to overcome all the power of the enemy; nothing will harm you. However, do not rejoice that the spirits submit to you, but rejoice that your names are written in Heaven.'" Luke 10:18-20 (NIV)

Satan was the highest angel in Heaven, but his pride got him cast out. He wanted to be God instead of a servant of God. He acts as the leader of the fallen angels. He masquerades as an angel of light, deceiving God's children. Learn who you are in Christ so you aren't easily deceived. As God's child, you are given authority over the enemy. Do not fall into anger and depression when you're under attack, but instead use your power to overcome the enemy.

Christ's Power Rests On You

———◆———

"But He said to me, 'My grace is sufficient for you, for My power is made perfect in weakness.' Therefore I will boast all the more gladly about my weaknesses, so that Christ's power may rest on me." 2 Corinthians 12:9 (NIV)

There's not one person who doesn't struggle with weaknesses. It may not be the same weakness someone else struggles with, but we all have weaknesses. Your weakness isn't necessarily a bad thing. If you had no weaknesses, you wouldn't feel the need to depend on God's power daily. Your weaknesses allow God to show Himself strong in your life. He is using your transformation to bring others closer to Him. God gives us choices. You can choose to rely on your own strength to fight your weaknesses or you can choose to rely on God's power and strength!

Worrying Can't Change Anything

"Which of you by worrying can add one cubit to his stature?"
Matthew 6:27 (NKJV)

As you pursue your dreams, it's hard not to worry. You continually pray for situations to turn out the way you hoped, but fortunately we don't always get our way. God is taking you the best way, but you have to trust Him. Life won't always look the way you imagined. You can only see the next step in front of you, but keep walking by faith. God takes you through a process first. The process is strengthening you for your destination. The bigger the promise, the bigger the problems so be sure to appreciate where you are now and how far you've come. Worrying only kills your spirit and it won't change anything. Continue moving forward with gratitude, walking in perfect peace!

God Made You Wonderful

"For You created my inmost being; You knit me together in my mother's womb. I praise You because I am fearfully and wonderfully made; Your works are wonderful, I know that full well." Psalm 139:13-14 (NIV)

You are made with a uniqueness. You weren't created by God to be like someone else. There may be qualities you have that make you feel like you don't belong or that make you feel different from all the other people around you. It makes you feel uncomfortable at times, but that's because it's true. You are different and you don't fit in, but you weren't made to fit in. God created you to stand out from the crowd. He gave you gifts that set you apart from your friends and family. Explore the many gifts God placed deep down inside of you and embrace your uniqueness!

Nothing Is Too Hard For God

---◆---

"Then the Lord said to Abraham, 'Why did Sarah laugh and say, 'Will I really have a child, now that I am old?' Is anything too hard for the Lord? I will return to you at the appointed time next year, and Sarah will have a son.'"
Genesis 18:13-14 (NIV)

It doesn't matter how old you are when God decides to use you. Some people feel like it's too late to go after their dream, but there is nothing God can't do. He decided which gifts would be placed within you. God also chooses the perfect moment for you to give birth to each gift. Your gifts will be drawn out and revealed one gift at a time as you continue learning who you were created to be. Never let anyone deceive you by telling you it's too late to accomplish your mission. Figure out your purpose and PURSUE IT!

You Reap What You Sow

———⊰◆⊱———

"Do not be deceived: God cannot be mocked. A man reaps what he sows. Whoever sows to please their flesh, from the flesh will reap destruction; whoever sows to please the Spirit, from the Spirit will reap eternal life." Galatians 6:7-8 (NIV)

You can't pretend or hide from God. He sees everything you do. If you follow what your flesh wants, trouble will eventually come. We are all sinful by nature which is why our flesh will lead us into destruction. It's very important to please the Spirit and not your flesh. Your flesh leads you to sin and your sin leads you to eternal death. The Spirit will lead you to eternal life. Please remember that you get back whatever you put out. Let the Spirit guide you and bless you with perfect peace. Let the Spirit fill you with joy which will strengthen you!

We Have All Sinned

"When they kept on questioning Him, He straightened up and said to them, 'Let any one of you who is without sin be the first to throw a stone at her.'" John 8:7 (NIV)

Be careful of judging other people because you never know what they are going through in their private lives. Sometimes God will put you in the same predicament to allow you to experience what someone else is struggling with. If you want grace for your sins, be gracious toward other people when they sin. Judging the other person will only hurt them and make them more distant from God. Instead of judging them, take them by the hand and help them get up. Build them up and allow them to see God within you. Encouraging someone who has fallen will help strengthen them and eventually bring them closer to God.

Satan Is The Father Of Lies

⇒•◇•⇐

"You belong to your father, the devil, and you want to carry out your father's desires. He was a murderer from the beginning, not holding to the truth, for there is no truth in him. When he lies, he speaks his native language, for he is a liar and the father of lies." John 8:44 (NIV)

As you continue on your journey toward your purpose, you will experience different attacks from Satan. The closer you get to your destiny, the stronger the attacks will be. Satan will do all he can to distract you. He uses people or whatever he can to take your peace. When you're under attack, use the power God has given you. God is all powerful and He lives within you. Take authority over Satan. Rejoice because you know that the stronger the attack, the closer you are to your destiny!

Your Reward Is In Heaven

———◆———

"Blessed are you when people insult you, persecute you and falsely say all kinds of evil against you because of Me. Rejoice and be glad, because great is your reward in Heaven, for in the same way they persecuted the prophets who were before you." Matthew 5:11-12 (NIV)

There are people who hate you for the light that shines brightly through you because of God's Spirit within you. Your light is irritating to certain people because it brings out guilt within them and reminds them of how evil their deeds are as they continue to live in darkness. People may persecute you because they can't stand to see how blessed you are. God makes it clear that you're blessed when people insult you because of Him. He tells you to rejoice because He has a great reward for you in Heaven!

Fear Nothing

———◦◦◦———

"The Lord is my light and my salvation, whom shall I fear? The Lord is the stronghold of my life, of whom shall I be afraid?" Psalm 27:1 (NIV)

Fear can be very paralyzing. It can keep you from going after what's yours. The enemy will use different tactics to keep you stuck in one place, but you have a power within you that is all powerful. The Lord's power trumps any spirit of fear. Overcome the spirit of fear by praying to the Lord constantly. If you feel anxiety coming on, immediately start praying. You'll be surprised at what you can accomplish once you learn your power in Christ. Without fear, you would probably try doing everything in your own power which can tire you out. So allow your fear to work for you by bringing you closer to Christ who can do all things!

God Will Provide

"Therefore I tell you, do not worry about your life, what you will eat or drink; or about your body, what you will wear. Is not life more than food, and the body more than clothes? Look at the birds of the air; they do not sow or reap or store away in barns, and yet your Heavenly Father feeds them. Are you not much more valuable than they?" Matthew 6:25-26 (NIV)

Your Father is the Creator of all things. He provides all things. Your faith may be tested at times to see how much you truly trust Him. You won't always have what you want, but if you are a good steward over what God has given you, He will bless you more abundantly. Remain grateful and humble as God provides for you. Give to others who are in need and God will reward you for your sacrifice.

God Is Your Foundation

"Therefore everyone who hears these words of Mine and puts them into practice is like a wise man who built his house on the rock. The rain came down, the streams rose, and the winds blew and beat against that house; yet it did not fall, because it had its foundation on the rock." Matthew 7:24-25 (NIV)

It's good to study the Word, but if you want to be transformed then you need to practice what you learn. God will teach you through the Holy Spirit and allow you to take the test. He gives you a chance to practice what you're learning. Pay close attention and stay focused. When storms come to destroy you, it won't take you down because of the strength God's Word has given you. God is your rock! A storm will only strengthen you for the next level as you remain in Christ.

The Holy Spirit Lives Within You

"And I will ask the Father, and He will give you another advocate to help you and be with you forever— the Spirit of Truth. The world cannot accept Him, because it neither sees Him nor knows Him. But you know Him, for He lives with you and will be in you." John 14:16-17 (NIV)

God chooses who He will to do His work. He comes to you when you least expect it. When God chooses you, He won't make you follow Him. He gives you free will to choose Him or the world. When you're chosen by God, He will give you eyes to see Him and ears to hear Him. Realize how truly special and blessed you are when you're chosen by the Almighty God. Allow Him to use you mightily in His Kingdom to bring many more souls to Him as possible before He comes back. Be obedient and answer God's call.

Jesus Is Our Physician

━━◆◇◆━━

"When the Pharisees saw this, they asked His disciples, 'Why does your teacher eat with tax collectors and sinners?' On hearing this, Jesus said, 'It is not the healthy who need a doctor, but the sick.'" Matthew 9:11-12 (NIV)

If you're a disciple of Christ, follow His example. Jesus didn't keep a wall up between Him and sinners. He actually socialized with them and broke down many walls. Jesus explained that it is the ones who are sick that need a physician. Don't allow your friends or associates to make you feel bad about socializing with people who are walking down the wrong path because those are the ones who need Christ. Keep in mind that you can't help who you refuse to touch or talk to. Be open to spreading God's love to everyone God has brought into your life.

Jesus Brings Calmness

———◆———

"Suddenly a furious storm came up on the lake, so that the waves swept over the boat. But Jesus was sleeping. The disciples went and woke Him, saying, 'Lord, save us! We're going to drown!' He replied, 'You of little faith, why are you so afraid?' Then He got up and rebuked the winds and the waves, and it was completely calm." Matthew 8:24-26 (NIV)

Storms will rise up to test your faith. Jesus is the perfect example of how we ought to be when trouble comes. Instead of Jesus being fearful of what was happening in the storm, He slept through it. He remained calm and rebuked the storm. Jesus is teaching you how to use the power and authority within you. Use the power God gave you and continue on in faith remembering that all things are working together for a bigger purpose. When storms break out remain calm and use your God-given power.

The Peace Within Your Heart

—◆—

"A sound heart is the life of the flesh: but envy the rottenness of the bones." Proverbs 14:30 (KJV)

Followers of Christ are blessed with a peace which surpasses all understanding. It doesn't matter what's happening around you because of the strength and peace God gives His children. A child of God can withstand any attack from Satan if they remain close to God. If you're envious of your brother, it only destroys you as a person. The bitterness will eat away at your spirit and weaken you. Be at peace with everyone God brings into your life. We are all just trying to find our way Home to our Heavenly Father. Help your brother if they're falling instead of kicking them while they're down. The more unified we are, the harder it is for Satan to steal another soul from God's Kingdom.

Rewarded According to Deeds

"The heart is deceitful above all things and beyond cure. Who can understand it? 'I the Lord search the heart and examine the mind, to reward each person according to their conduct, according to what their deeds deserve.'" Jeremiah 17:9-10 (NIV)

As a human being you are naturally sinful, but God knows your heart. There's nothing you can hide from Him. You have to make a decision to follow what the Holy Spirit is leading you to do or you could fall into Satan's trap. Remember that you are rewarded for your deeds whether they are good or bad. If you choose to do good deeds, your reward will be good. If you choose to do evil deeds, God will forgive you, but you still have to pay for the bad you chose to do. Continue to do good works and receive great rewards from the Lord.

Your Eyes And Ears Are Blessed

"But blessed are your eyes because they see, and your ears because they hear. For truly I tell you, many prophets and righteous people longed to see what you see but did not see it, and to hear what you hear but did not hear it." Matthew 13:16-17 (NIV)

God chose you while living in darkness and gave you light. There are people in your life that were expecting you not to make it. God chose to transform you to allow others to see how real He is and to believe in Him. God stepped into your life to do a mighty miracle. You are blessed to be chosen by God to see Him and to hear Him. Some of the most "holy" people can't see what you see or hear what you hear. Remain grateful and humble as God uses you to do mighty works in His Kingdom!

Do Not Doubt The Lord

"Come," He said. Then Peter got down out of the boat, walked on the water and came toward Jesus. But when he saw the wind, he was afraid and, beginning to sink, cried out, "Lord, save me!" Immediately Jesus reached out His hand and caught him. "You of little faith," He said, "why did you doubt?" Matthew 14:29-31 (NIV)

When God calls you to Him, there will be storms that rise up to make you doubt your call. Your faith will be strengthened during these storms once you realize that God is with you and He won't allow you to drown in the storm. God has a purpose for you, but the storms are necessary to strengthen you as a person. The storms bring out what God put deep down inside of you. They teach you what you are truly made of. Don't allow the storm to drown you, but fight harder since you know that there is always a lesson in the storm and a blessing after the storm. When storms break out in your life, get excited because they are opportunities to workout your faith in Christ and to learn more about who God created you to be in His Kingdom.

Follow God's Example

———◆———

"Follow God's example, therefore, as dearly loved children and walk in the way of love, just as Christ loved us and gave Himself up for us as a fragrant offering and sacrifice to God."
Ephesians 5:1-2 (NIV)

It is not enough to claim to be God's child and to talk about God's love. It's not what you say that matters most, it's what you do. Are you showing God's love through action? Jesus doesn't just tell people He loves them. Jesus shows people through His actions that He loves them. As God's child, you are not to only talk about your love for others, but also show them by living continuously in love. God shows His love for us by His constant sacrifice. What sacrifices are you making to show your love for God and for other people?

Who Is Wise Among You?

"Who is wise and understanding among you? Let them show it by their good life, by deeds done in the humility that comes from wisdom." James 3:13 (NIV)

It's important as a child of God to live righteously. You don't always have to witness to others with words. As you live righteously, do good deeds, and remain humble, it will inspire others to live the same way. People will want to know what your secret is that keeps you living righteously. This will open up an opportunity to witness to those around you about Jesus Christ. God will continue to fill you with wisdom as you remain in Him. He will teach you about all things as you grow in Him. Continue living a quiet, humble life as you sacrifice all you can to help grow God's Kingdom.

Don't Lose Your Soul

⊰⬥⊱

"For what is a man profited, if he shall gain the whole world, and lose his own soul? Or what shall a man give in exchange for his soul?" Matthew 16:26 (KJV)

There will be opportunities that present themselves to you as you go after your purpose. Be sure that the opportunity is of God. Satan is smooth and he will promise you the whole world to follow his ways. Satan will offer you things that are hard to exist, but those things will not save you in the end. There's nothing in this world that is worth more than your soul. If you died right now, your money or possessions would not matter since you can't take it with you. Go after your dreams, using discernment. God offers something money could never buy. He offers an eternity filled with love, peace, joy, and so much more.

God Rejoices When We Return

"What do you think? If a man owns a hundred sheep, and one of them wanders away, will he not leave the ninety-nine on the hills and go to look for the one that wandered off? And if he finds it, truly I tell you, he is happier about that one sheep than about the ninety-nine that did not wander off." Matthew 18:12-13 (NIV)

If you backslide and fall away from God, He will find ways to bring you back to Him. He will put people in your path to speak with you or allow you to see signs all around you reminding you that you are His and He loves you unconditionally. When God brings you back into His family, He rejoices along with His angels. All of Heaven celebrates when one of His children comes back to Him. You are blessed to be loved by the Creator of Heaven and earth.

God Is In The Midst Of Us

⟾⬥⬥⟽

"Again, truly I tell you that if two of you on earth agree about anything they ask for, it will be done for them by My Father in Heaven. For where two or three gather in My name, there am I with them." Matthew 18:19-20 (NIV)

Pray with your brothers and sisters believing God will make it happen. Jesus is letting you know that when you pray with others in His name, He will be in the midst of you all. He will give you what you are asking for when you touch and agree with your brothers or sisters. Pray often with the people you love. Our journeys can get pretty tough at times, which is why you need brothers and sisters that you trust who are strong in prayer. Be grateful when God blesses you with a prayer warrior in your life to face all that will come on your journey.

Live Your Life Using Wisdom

"Be very careful, then, how you live—not as unwise but as wise, making the most of every opportunity, because the days are evil." Ephesians 5:15-16 (NIV)

If you pay attention to the world around you, you'll realize that a lot of the things happening right now indicates we are living in the end times. No one knows the last day or hour, but the signs are all around us. Don't waste another day being unproductive. Live wisely listening to the Holy Spirit and following His guidance. When the Holy Spirit guides you into an opportunity, be grateful and make the most of it. Don't regret anything that happens in your life because all things are working together for your good. You are still in the process of becoming the great man or woman God created you to be. Stay focused!

Be Slow To Become Angry

―――◆―――

"My dear brothers and sisters, take note of this: Everyone should be quick to listen, slow to speak and slow to become angry, because human anger does not produce the righteousness that God desires." James 1:19-20 (NIV)

It's not easy to remain in a state of tranquility, especially when you're agitated about where you are in life right now. When you know you were created for something bigger and you're trying to find your true purpose in life, anything can upset you if you're feeling stuck. God has you where He needs you to be right now to produce patience, self-control, self-discipline, and to strengthen you for the next level. When you're feeling agitated, don't be so quick to fly off the handle. Take a moment to calm down and pray. Ask God for peace and guidance.

God Gave You Sight

—❖—

"Jesus stopped and called them. 'What do you want Me to do for you?' He asked. 'Lord,' they answered, 'we want our sight.' Jesus had compassion on them and touched their eyes. Immediately they received their sight and followed Him."
Matthew 20:32-34 (NIV)

God will meet you in the darkest moments in your life. He goes out of His way to bring you to Him. He wants to give you life and fill you with His love. He wants to open your eyes so you can see Him. Don't hide from Him. He doesn't care about your past or what you're into now. He just wants to bring you Home to Him and have a genuine relationship with you. God says come as you are. He wants you to receive your sight so that you can see Him. When He opens your eyes, continue to follow Him! Your eyes are now opened!

God Gives You Strength

———◈———

"But the Lord stood at my side and gave me strength, so that through me the message might be fully proclaimed and all the Gentiles might hear it. And I was delivered from the lion's mouth." 2 Timothy 4:17 (NIV)

God brings you out of things that would've destroyed you or swallowed you whole. As a child of God's, you're protected from whatever threatens to take you under. As you face trials, God reminds you that He is right there with you. God is strengthening you for the battle you face right now. Once He saves you from this battle, He will use you as a vessel to strengthen others who are hurting by spreading His message and giving your testimony. Be grateful that He chose you for a time such as this, for such a great mission in His mighty Kingdom. Give it all you got!

The Young And The Old

⟫◈⟪

"The glory of young men is their strength: and the beauty of old men is the grey head." Proverbs 20:29 (KJV)

We are facing hard times around the world right now. Things are getting scary, but we have each other. God uses older people in His Kingdom to spread wisdom. They've seen a lot in their time here on earth. They have experiences that young people don't have in certain situations. When an elder is talking to you about their experiences, open your ears. One of the most powerful ways to gain wisdom is learning how to listen. The more you learn, the more power you gain. We need the wisdom of older people and the strength of younger people to accomplish great missions in order to bring as many people into God's Kingdom as possible before Christ returns.

God Exalts The Humble

—◆◆◆—

"The greatest among you will be your servant. For those who exalt themselves will be humbled, and those who humble themselves will be exalted." Matthew 23:11-12 (NIV)

God will draw you to Him and transform you for His glory. He will use you as a servant to serve His people. Be careful not to fall into pride as you are being used in God's Kingdom. Before a fall comes pride so remain humble and God will lift you up. It's easier to remain humble when you're filled with gratitude for all God has brought you through. Always remember that you're able to do what you do because of God's power within you. The moment you forget that God's in control and work in your own power, you will tire out. Be humble as God takes you higher remembering He is the reason for your success.

Work Hard For The Lord

"Who then is the faithful and wise servant, whom the Master has put in charge of the servants in His household to give them their food at the proper time? It will be good for that servant whose Master finds him doing so when He returns. Truly I tell you, He will put him in charge of all His possessions."
Matthew 24:45-47 (NIV)

God chose you to work in His Kingdom. Study God's Word to gain wisdom and remain faithful as you serve His children. Jesus will be coming back, but none of us know the exact day or hour. It's important to do the Lord's work daily so that when Christ returns, He will find you working hard for the Kingdom. God will bless and reward you for all that you're doing in His Kingdom. Work hard and serve the people of God like today was your last day.

Christ Laid Down His Life

⟫◆⟪

"This is how we know what love is: Jesus Christ laid down His life for us. And we ought to lay down our lives for our brothers and sisters." 1 John 3:16 (NIV)

You may say you love someone, but what do your actions say? Jesus actually sacrificed everything He had to save you. Can you think of a greater sacrifice of love than laying down your life for your brother or sister? How many can truly say that if they were confronted with death and had to make a choice between their life or their loved one's life, would actually choose to sacrifice their own life? Talk is just talk. Show your love to your loved ones with action. Don't just talk, but be willing to sacrifice your time when they are needing you. Be more like Jesus and love others unconditionally.

Ask For God's Will To Be Done

"Going a little farther, He fell with His face to the ground and prayed, 'My Father, if it is possible, may this cup be taken from Me. Yet not as I will, but as You will.'" Matthew 26:39 (NIV)

Jesus shows us the perfect way we ought to pray when we come to God. Although Jesus knew He came to save us all from eternal death, He still asked God to take the bitter cup away from Him. He knew the suffering He would endure before He gave His life to save us from eternal death. At the end of the prayer, Jesus asked for God's will to be done and not His own. When you pray, do you ask God for His will to be done or do you want what you want even if it's not the best for you? Pray for what you're wanting, but always keep in mind that God's will and way is the best way!

Show Hospitality To All People

—◇—

"Do not forget to show hospitality to strangers, for by so doing some people have shown hospitality to angels without knowing it." Hebrews 13:2 (NIV)

Wherever you go and whoever you meet, be the person God is shaping you to be. Be loving, kind, and compassionate toward others. You could be taking a test when God brings certain people in your path to see how you treat others who don't look like you or act like you. Be careful in the way you respond to others because it could be an angel of God that you're entertaining. You will get back what you give out. Treat others the way you would like to be treated no matter what they look like, dress like, or even smell like. Be loving and kind to all people.

The Spirit Of God Rests On You

———◆———

"If you are insulted because of the name of Christ, you are blessed, for the Spirit of glory and of God rests on you." 1 Peter 4:14 (NIV)

God will lead you into certain places to minister to other people, but everyone won't receive you with open arms. Some people will be irritated by your messages from God, but celebrate realizing that Jesus was persecuted first. You are blessed whenever people persecute you because of Christ's name. God's glory and light is all over you. You are blessed to be chosen by the Most High to be used as a vessel to spread the Word of God. Rejoice in the Lord for pouring out His Spirit and His favor over you as you continue on your journey.

JUNE 23ʳᵈ

God Provides All You Need

———◆———

"And God is able to bless you abundantly, so that in all things at all times, having all that you need, you will abound in every good work." 2 Corinthians 9:8 (NIV)

God will do your work if you do His work. When you work for God and allow Him to use you in His Kingdom, He will bless you with more than you could ever ask. Every need you have, God already knows about it. As you trust Him fully, He will pour out His abundance over you. He takes great care of His children. It may not be in the way you expected, but stop worrying and know that all your needs will be met as you follow God. You can live in perfect peace since you know that God is holding you in His hand and He will not allow you to fall. Do not worry about anything today. God has already worked it all out.

Gossip Can Be Hurtful

＝＞◆＜＝

"The words of a talebearer are as wounds, and they go down into the innermost parts of the belly." Proverbs 26:22 (KJV)

You may tell yourself, "I'm not going to gossip about others today." Next thing you know, you may be the main one gossiping that day. It's always funny when you're gossiping about others, but if you find out someone was gossiping about you, things get more serious. You don't realize how hurtful gossiping can be until God allows you to be on the other end and experience how painful it can be when you're the one being talked about. Once you fall into gossip, it's easier for a spirit of negativity to take over. It won't be an easy task, but if you realize a spirit of gossip taking over your conversation with your loved ones, remove yourself from the situation.

God Will Be With You

$\Longrightarrow\!\!\Leftrightarrow\!\!\Longleftarrow$

"Have I not commanded you? Be strong and courageous. Do not be afraid; do not be discouraged, for the LORD your God will be with you wherever you go." Joshua 1:9 (NIV)

As you continue walking with the Lord, your fear will start to dissipate. The closer you get to Christ, the stronger you become in your spirit. As you become stronger, you are able to accomplish great goals because of your fearlessness. God is strengthening you as you walk with Him and trust Him. It's God's power within you that allows you to do the Lord's work. Wherever you're being led, be courageous since you know that God stays close to His children. He's with you as you go after your calling. Things won't always work the way you planned, but don't get discouraged. God is with you at all times!

Speak God's Name Without Fear

———⟨◇⟩———

"Then they called them in again and commanded them not to speak or teach at all in the name of Jesus. But Peter and John replied, 'Which is right in God's eyes: to listen to you, or to Him? You be the judges! As for us, we cannot help speaking about what we have seen and heard.'" Acts 4:18-20 (NIV)

Do not be afraid to speak the name of Jesus no matter what anyone tries to threaten you with. God is the One you will have to answer to when you pass from this physical world. Your life here on earth is temporary, but Heaven is forever. Do what's right in God's sight, not men. God will bless you for your boldness to speak the name of Jesus freely! Jesus reveals Himself to whomever He chooses. After He shows Himself to you, it's hard not to tell others what He's shown you.

The Blind Cannot Lead The Blind

"Leave them; they are blind guides. If the blind lead the blind, both will fall into a pit." Matthew 15:14 (NIV)

Two blind people can't lead each other. Keep people around you who are moving upward. If you're already feeling lost and don't know where to go in life, it will only get worse if you're being led by someone who is just as lost as you are. You will both fall into a downward spiral. Surround yourself with people who are going after positive things and who are speaking positively. It's easy to adopt the ways of others if you're around them constantly so be sure to hang around people who are motivating and inspirational allowing you both to soar higher. Be nice to all people, but be cautious of who you are spending the majority of your time with.

JUNE 28TH

What Is Stored Up In Your Heart?

"A good man brings good things out of the good stored up in his heart, and an evil man brings evil things out of the evil stored up in his heart. For the mouth speaks what the heart is full of." Luke 6:45 (NIV)

Use discernment while you're with people. Listen to the things a person says while you're around them. Pay attention to the way they treat others. You will know more about a person by what comes out of their mouths. Don't be fooled. If a person tells you who they are, believe them. Pray that God will transform them, but also protect your heart from any evil that may be spewing from their heart. Show people the goodness within your own heart by being an encourager who builds people up with the words God has blessed you with through the Holy Spirit to help others.

Keep Your Eyes On The Lord

"I keep my eyes always on the Lord. With Him at my right hand, I will not be shaken." Psalm 16:8 (NIV)

Satan sends distractions your way to take your focus off Jesus. He uses people to take you out of character. Satan will keep you so busy that your mind loses peace. He sends storms your way to distract you from your calling, but remain still and allow God to fight your battles. Put your complete trust in God knowing He won't allow Satan to shake you in this storm. God has His army of angels encamped all around you. When your enemies surround you, God surrounds your enemies. God will give you the victory over any enemies or storms that rise against you. There's no reason to be afraid when you have the Most High on your side. Truth is on your side and it shall prevail.

JUNE 30ᵀᴴ

Be A Trustworthy Person

"A gossip betrays a confidence, but a trustworthy person keeps a secret." Proverbs 11:13 (NIV)

If someone confides in you about something personal and they ask you to keep it to yourself, respect their wishes. When you talk about other people's business, it becomes gossip. Gossip can cause lots of friction. It can actually tear relationships apart. Think about how you felt the last time someone told something personal about you. Gossiping can put a wedge between you and your loved ones. Always be aware of the hurt that your words may cause someone else. Unless you're intervening to keep someone safe, keep their secrets to yourself. Gossip is more serious than it may seem. People have taken their own lives because of gossiping. Be trustworthy to your friends and family.

God's Chosen Instrument

—⟫⬧⟪—

"But the Lord said to Ananias, 'Go! This man is My chosen instrument to proclaim My name to the Gentiles and their kings and to the people of Israel. I will show him how much he must suffer for My name.'" Acts 9:15-16 (NIV)

God chose to use you in His Kingdom. Things may seem awkward at first when you don't understand it. God is walking you through it. He is blessing you with wisdom as you stay close to Him. Satan will put people in your path along the way to confuse you. Stay focused and aware of your surroundings. As you grow in Christ, God uses you to reach others who are lost. You will suffer for His name, but keep in mind God tells us we're blessed when we suffer for His name. Remain strong in Christ as He fills you with power to fight battles for His namesake.

All Things Work Together

---◆---

"And we know that in all things God works for the good of those who love Him, who have been called according to His purpose." Romans 8:28 (NIV)

God formed you before He put you on this earth. He has already written your story from beginning to end. He has chosen to use you for a special purpose. Keep following Him and looking to Him for your purpose to be revealed. As you follow Him into your destiny, He will provide all you need to do all He has called you to do. There is no reason to worry about how you will make it. He has it all worked out and ready for you. Just love Him, trust Him, and remain in Him. God is keeping a hedge of protection around you. He has everything you need waiting for you as you reach the next level. Walk closely with God as He guides you.

Walk On In Freedom

———◆———

"And I will walk at liberty: for I seek thy precepts." Psalm 119:45 (KJV)

As you continue walking with Christ, He will teach you through His Holy Spirit. God is filling you with His love, light, and power through the Word. It's important to get God's Word in you daily. His Word is what begins to transform you into the person He created you to be before the beginning of time. You will learn who you were created to be the more you learn about your Creator. You will feel such a great freedom the closer you get to Christ. Even when Satan attacks you on every side, you can still have perfect peace as you trust in the One who Created you. God is teaching you right now what to do in every battle. Stand still as He fights for you and remain fully free in Christ.

Give God The Glory

"On the appointed day Herod, wearing his royal robes, sat on his throne and delivered a public address to the people. They shouted, 'This is the voice of a god, not of a man.' Immediately, because Herod did not give praise to God, an angel of the Lord struck him down, and he was eaten by worms and died." Acts 12:21-23 (NIV)

God will give you certain assignments He wants you to complete in order to bless His people, but always be sure to give God the glory instead of taking credit for yourself. Acknowledge God in all your success. It's God's power that allows you to do all you're doing. If people are praising you, direct their attention back to God since you know that all you're doing wouldn't be possible without God. Give God the glory in all He has blessed you to do.

You Can't Hide From God's Truth

―――・◇・―――

"But the Jewish leaders incited the God-fearing women of high standing and the leading men of the city. They stirred up persecution against Paul and Barnabas, and expelled them from their region. So they shook the dust off their feet as a warning to them and went to Iconium. And the disciples were filled with joy and with the Holy Spirit." Acts 13:50-52 (NIV)

Everyone won't accept the truth. People are afraid of the truth. If you speak the truth, they push you away. People have a hard time accepting truth because it means they have to change. Changing isn't easy, but it's necessary. For some people it's easier to hide from truth, but there will come a time no one will be able to hide from God's truth. Don't be one of the ones who wait until it's too late to accept the truth.

Value The Interests Of Others

"Do nothing out of selfish ambition or vain conceit. Rather, in humility value others above yourselves, not looking to your own interests but each of you to the interests of the others." Philippians 2:3-4 (NIV)

You will strengthen your relationships when you put your own interests to the side to help your brother or sister with their interests. When you humbly value the interest of someone else and help that person accomplish their goals, God will help you accomplish your goals. Put away any kind of selfishness and value what someone else values. There is fulfillment in helping others reach their goals. You gain more peace and power when you can be of assistance to another person by helping them fulfill their dreams. Who can you help accomplish their mission?

Use Your Freedom To Serve

"You, my brothers and sisters, were called to be free. But do not use your freedom to indulge the flesh; rather, serve one another humbly in love." Galatians 5:13 (NIV)

You were chosen by God to come out of darkness and to walk in freedom. You weren't created to live in bondage. Do not be fooled by the devil and his traps. Everything that feels good to your flesh is not good. Your own fleshy desires will make you a slave to the devil and will trap you in a life of sin. Your flesh will crave things that aren't good for your spirit. Different things may feel good to your flesh in the moment, but later on guilt kicks in making you fall into depression. Stay free from sin as you love others and serve others. Enjoy living in freedom and enjoy perfect peace as you walk with the Lord.

God Freed You From Bondage

⟶◈⟵

"About midnight, Paul and Silas were praying and singing hymns to God, and the other prisoners were listening to them. Suddenly there was such a violent earthquake that the foundations of the prison were shaken. At once all the prison doors flew open, and everyone's chains came loose." Acts 16:25-26 (NIV)

God will call you into places that seem unbearable. When He brings you into a hard situation, it's not always about you. God will use your hardships to bring Himself glory and to bring others out of bondage. Pray to God and celebrate God in the midst of your trouble. Allow others to see that when you celebrate God in trouble, He will break every chain off of you and loose you. When others see what God brought you out of, they will also come to God for deliverance.

God Will Protect You From Harm

—◆—

"One night the Lord spoke to Paul in a vision: 'Do not be afraid; keep on speaking, do not be silent. For I am with you, and no one is going to attack and harm you, because I have many people in this city.'" Acts 18:9-10 (NIV)

God will speak to you in all kinds of ways, through all kinds of people. Keep your eyes and ears open to what the Lord is telling you. Test the spirits whenever someone speaks into your life. Be sure it is of God. Go boldly into the world teaching others what God is teaching you in your alone time with Him. Ask the Holy Spirit for guidance before you start your day. Speak without fear of anyone. God is bringing you into new territory to spread His Word. Don't be afraid since you know God is with you wherever you go. He has His people around you.

The Spirit Of God Is Freedom

"Now the Lord is that Spirit, and where the Spirit of the Lord is, there is liberty." 2 Corinthians 3:17 (KJV)

When you come to God, He fills you with the Holy Spirit. The Holy Spirit is your guide. He intercedes to protect you from harm. If you have feelings about certain people or places, listen to those feelings. The Holy Spirit is warning you, but it's your choice to listen or not. Your way can get you into trouble. Your way can trap you in situations that are painful, but the Holy Spirit's way leads you to freedom. Wherever the Holy Spirit leads you, rest easy knowing that He is bringing you into a place of serenity. You are not alone. God is right there with you wanting to guide you. Make a choice right now. Will you let Him lead you to freedom and perfect peace?

The Salt Of The Earth

—⟫◆⟪—

"You are the salt of the earth. But if the salt loses its saltiness, how can it be made salty again? It is no longer good for anything, except to be thrown out and trampled underfoot."
Matthew 5:13 (NIV)

You were given a position in God's Kingdom. You were chosen by God to make a difference here on earth. It's important to use your position of power to influence those God has given you to influence. When God puts you in position, don't misuse your power and influence. If you take advantage of your position, your influence on others will fade. You will lose the position God has given you. There's no point in God keeping you in your position if you're no longer of any use to Him in the Kingdom. When God blesses you with an opportunity and position, don't blow it!

Be On Your Guard

—◦◦◦—

"I know that after I leave, savage wolves will come in among you and will not spare the flock. Even from your own number men will arise and distort the truth in order to draw away disciples after them. So be on your guard! Remember that for three years I never stopped warning each of you night and day with tears." Acts 20:29-31 (NIV)

When you get a word from God, Satan will do all he can to make you doubt it. Don't be deceived. Trust what God says believing it will come to pass. It takes great faith to believe God in the midst of trouble, but God can't lie. Sometimes people you trust will rise up and tell a lie on you. Keep your eyes open and remember not to put all your trust in people. They're only human and we all make mistakes as human beings. Trust God fully and what He is telling you.

The Enemy Will Come Back

———◆———

"And when the devil had ended all the temptation, he departed from Him for a season." Luke 4:13 (KJV)

Stay alert at all times because Satan desires to have all God's children. The devil will deceive you in any way he can. It's important to know yourself inside and out. What are your weaknesses? What tempts you constantly? The devil will wait patiently to tempt you with evil. He will wait until you feel like you're on top of the world, then he comes to entice you with pride, greedy desires, and entitlement. Be careful not to fall into the traps Satan sets for your feet. Satan will wait until you are overwhelmed or tired to tempt you with evil desires. Stay alert, stay prayed up, and stay focused with your eyes on the Lord at all times!

JULY 14TH

Write Your Vision Down

———❖———

"Then the Lord answered me and said: 'Write the vision and make it plain on tablets, that he may run who reads it. For the vision is yet for an appointed time; but at the end it will speak, and it will not lie. Though it tarries, wait for it; because it will surely come, it will not tarry.'" Habakkuk 2:2-3 (NKJV)

When God gives you a vision, make it plain on paper so that when you die your vision will live on through the next generations. Be patient as you work for your vision to come to pass. You may not see it come to pass, but your children's children will see it and have something to fall back on. What you do today will determine the kind of future your children will have. Keep in mind that a person with no vision will eventually return to their past. Stay focused!

It's Better To Give Than Receive

—⊰◈⊱—

"I have not coveted anyone's silver or gold or clothing. You yourselves know that these hands of mine have supplied my own needs and the needs of my companions. In everything I did, I showed you that by this kind of hard work we must help the weak, remembering the words the Lord Jesus Himself said: 'It is more blessed to give than to receive.'" Acts 20:33-35 (NIV)

If there's someone you know who needs help, let them see the God within you by helping them. Don't always be ready to receive more than you are willing to give. As you take care of God's people, God will also take care of you. God is the reason you are blessed to have what you have. God gave it to you, but He can also take it back. It's all God's anyway so if He puts it in your heart to help someone, do it!

The Lord's Will Be Done

"Then Paul answered, 'Why are you weeping and breaking my heart? I am ready not only to be bound, but also to die in Jerusalem for the name of the Lord Jesus.' When he would not be dissuaded, we gave up and said, 'The Lord's will be done.'" Acts 21:13-14 (NIV)

When you're chosen by God, be ready not only for great blessings, but also for persecution. Everyone won't be supportive of your beliefs or what God chose you to do, but trust the Lord. Don't let anyone dissuade you from what God put within you to do. You have to decide if you're going to be all the way with God or not. If opportunities arise and nothing happens with it, don't give up. Always pray for God's will to be done. Even if things are getting difficult, trust God's Holy Spirit to lead you, not people.

Coming Out Of Captivity

"But see, we are slaves today, slaves in the land You gave our ancestors so they could eat its fruit and the other good things it produces. Because of our sins, its abundant harvest goes to the kings You have placed over us. They rule over our bodies and our cattle as they please. We are in great distress." Nehemiah 9:36-37 (NIV)

God brings you out of captivity, but you have to play a part in your own freedom as well. If you fall back into sin, quickly repent and continue moving forward. There's a great harvest waiting for you on the other side of this battle. Go and get what God has just for you. It will get difficult at times, but the reward waiting for you on the other side of this battle will be worth every teardrop you cry. Ask God for strength in this battle.

Fix Your Eyes On The Lord

"Therefore, since we are surrounded by such a great cloud of witnesses, let us throw off everything that hinders and the sin that so easily entangles. And let us run with perseverance the race marked out for us, fixing our eyes on Jesus, the pioneer and perfecter of faith. For the joy set before Him He endured the cross, scorning its shame, and sat down at the right hand of the throne of God." Hebrews 12:1-2 (NIV)

People around you are watching the incredible transformation that is happening in your life and they want what you have. Allow them to see what it looks like when God pours out His love and grace over you as He brings you into His light. Battles come, but keep your eyes fixed on Jesus always remembering the sacrifice He made on the cross for your salvation.

God Is The Potter

"Woe to those who quarrel with their Maker, those who are nothing but potsherds among the potsherds on the ground. Does the clay say to the potter, 'What are you making?' Does your work say, 'The potter has no hands?'" Isaiah 45:9 (NIV)

When you're going through trials, it's hard not to question God. When you're being shaped in a specific area, it's painful. Some days you feel good about what God is doing in your life and then other days you start to wonder if God forgot to finish making you into the person He promised He would. God is taking you through the process. Process is never pretty, but it's necessary. Trust God when He is removing things or adding new things to your life. He will finish what He started in you. Trust Him even in the painful, messy parts.

God Will Lead You Out

"He led you through the vast and dreadful wilderness, that thirsty and waterless land, with its venomous snakes and scorpions. He brought you water out of hard rock." Deuteronomy 8:15 (NIV)

If you're losing hope because of the attacks coming at you on every side, remember all God has brought you through before. God didn't save you just to kick you to the curb. When you're feeling confused, reach out to God and ask Him what He wants from you. Are there any changes you need to make? God will show you what needs to change, but be open to His answer. Don't ask for help if you aren't willing to accept His truth. Sometimes God allows Satan to attack you in order to move you into a new thing. Don't stay somewhere God is trying to bring you out of. You might miss your blessing.

God Is Making A Way

—⟫◆⟪—

"Forget the former things; do not dwell on the past. See, I am doing a new thing! Now it springs up; do you not perceive it? I am making a way in the wilderness and streams in the wasteland." Isaiah 43:18-19 (NIV)

Do not harp on the past. There is nothing you can do to change it. The choices you make right now are what matters. When your situation starts to change, it can be overwhelming. Continue on in faith as God leads you to new heights. When God finds you faithful, He pours out His favor over you. He blesses all you do. As God leads the way, He provides all you need as you follow Him through the new doors He opens for you. God is holding you in His hand as He moves you to the next level and He will not let you fall. Trust God fully through this transition.

You Will Not Be Shaken

⟫⟩◆⟨⟪

"Those who trust in the Lord are like Mount Zion, which cannot be shaken but endures forever. As the mountains surround Jerusalem, so the Lord surrounds His people both now and forevermore." Psalm 125:1-2 (NIV)

Once you are chosen by God, He strengthens you and teaches you how to fight the enemy. Nothing will break you or move you out of the position God put you in. You're being strengthened at this very moment by God for the next level. The higher up you go, the stronger the attacks will be. Remain still since you know that when the enemy surrounds you, God surrounds your enemies. The attacks you experience will be painful, but it will not destroy you. God is on your side and nothing is more powerful than Him. Don't forget that Satan loses at the end of the story.

Receive The Crown Of Life

⟨≈⟩◆⟨≈⟩

"Blessed is the one who perseveres under trial because, having stood the test, that person will receive the crown of life that the Lord has promised to those who love Him." James 1:12 (NIV)

It's not a mistake that God placed you here on earth. You were created for a special purpose for a time such as this. Before you can understand what that purpose is, you will experience hardships. You will go through different tests and trials, but they are meant to strengthen you for whatever God has created you to do here on earth. Don't allow storms to devalue who God created you to be. He has a beautiful ending to your story if you remain close to Him. God blessed you with an overcomer spirit. You will overcome all Satan throws your way and God will bless you with the crown of life.

Do Not Become Easily Angered

---◆---

"And her rival also provoked her severely, to make her miserable, because the Lord had closed her womb." 1 Samuel 1:6 (NKJV)

There will be different seasons in your life. You have a planting season and a harvest season. You may not get what you've been praying for right away, but God knows the perfect time to bless you. Remain in peace when others are watching you and talking about your failures. Don't allow them to see you sweat if they start provoking you. God has already chosen to pour out His favor over you and to bless you. Be patient and wait for God's perfect timing. Once God opens the door to the next level, walk through it with class and perfect peace. You don't have to prove anything to anybody. God is your Father and He wants to give you the desires of your heart.

God Gives You Strength

"Do you not know? Have you not heard? The Lord is the everlasting God, the Creator of the ends of the earth. He will not grow tired or weary, and His understanding no one can fathom. He gives strength to the weary and increases the power of the weak." Isaiah 40:28-29 (NIV)

You're a child of God, which means you have His Spirit within you. God is all powerful and He lives within you. God will continue to be strong in you and He will continue to move through you to accomplish all He has called you to do. When the enemy is messing with your mind, use the power within you to take authority over the enemy. If you start to feel weak, take some time to sit alone with God. Ask God for the strength to keep going. The key to success is spending time with God everyday.

God Is Making Your Steps Firm

"The Lord makes firm the steps of the one who delights in Him; though he may stumble, he will not fall for the Lord upholds him with His hand." Psalm 37:23-24 (NIV)

The first half of your life won't look like the second half. When you're young, you don't know as much as you think you do. It's hard to understand the spiritual side of things until life brings you to your knees. Everyone eventually comes to a crossroads. You can choose to take God's path or the world's path. When you choose the world, you will trip over certain decisions you make in life. Although you may trip, God will not let you fall. Use your stumbling blocks as life lessons. Your life lessons will become the tools you need to make it to the next level in your life if you choose to learn from them.

Grace Is A Gift From God

"For it is by grace you have been saved, through faith—and this is not from yourselves, it is the gift of God—not by works, so that no one can boast." Ephesians 2:8-9 (NIV)

Not one of us is perfect. We have all sinned at some point in our lives. Salvation is not something that you can earn. God blessed us with a great gift to save us all. He blessed us with Jesus. If you believe in your heart and confess with your mouth that Jesus is the son of God, you are saved. Jesus died for us all because we all fall short of His glory. Don't let anyone convince you that you aren't good enough to receive salvation because God's Word tells us that none of us are good enough. Receive God's gift and live a life that shows your gratitude for the sacrifice Jesus made for us all.

Don't Forfeit Your Soul

"What good is it for someone to gain the whole world, yet forfeit their soul?" Mark 8:36 (NIV)

When you're God's child, there are many different things that can influence you while you're finding your way through life. Once you're closer to the top, remember who led you there and who will keep you there. Be careful not to fall into the traps of the enemy as he sets traps for your feet. Your flesh craves different things that are of the world. Anything that competes for your attention or steals your focus from God are considered to be of the world. Your soul is going to hell or to Heaven. It's your choice to suffer for eternity or live freely for eternity. The things of this world aren't worth holding on to if it takes your eyes off of God and takes your soul for eternity.

Have Compassion For Everyone

"Continue to remember those in prison as if you were together with them in prison, and those who are mistreated as if you yourselves were suffering." Hebrews 13:3 (NIV)

Everyone has different circumstances they face. You never know what someone else's struggles are or what their past was like until you listen to their life story. If someone is in prison that doesn't mean they're bad people. Learn to be more understanding of people and their situations. Be careful not to judge someone else. That's not your place. God will do the judging. We need only to do what God asked us to do. God wants us to remember those who are suffering and being mistreated in prison. You can't understand or help change who you refuse to talk to. We shouldn't be ok with losing any souls.

Do Not Waver In Your Belief

———◦◇◦———

"Yet he did not waver through unbelief regarding the promise of God, but was strengthened in his faith and gave glory to God, being fully persuaded that God had power to do what He had promised. This is why 'it was credited to him as righteousness.'" Romans 4:20-22 (NIV)

When God gives you a word, believe Him. He keeps His promises to the faithful. God will continue to show Himself faithful and will strengthen your faith as He fulfills all that He has told you. You will still experience hardships at times because they are the experiences that teaches you and strengthens you. As you walk through darker times, remember that God is with you and He will guide you with His light as you trust in Him fully. God will count your trust in Him as righteousness.

God Intercedes For His Children

<hr/>

"In the same way, the Spirit helps us in our weakness. We do not know what we ought to pray for, but the Spirit Himself intercedes for us through wordless groans. And He who searches our hearts knows the mind of the Spirit, because the Spirit intercedes for God's people in accordance with the will of God. And we know that in all things God works for the good of those who love Him, who have been called according to His purpose." Romans 8:26-28 (NIV)

You may not always know what to pray for in life, especially when you're going through down times. Remember when you're feeling lost that God's Spirit will intercede for you since you are His child. When certain circumstances come up that are painful, trust God to use all things and to make it work together for your good.

God's Mercy

———◆———

"What then shall we say? Is God unjust? Not at all! For He says to Moses, 'I will have mercy on whom I have mercy, and I will have compassion on whom I have compassion.' It does not, therefore, depend on human desire or effort, but on God's mercy." Romans 9:14-16 (NIV)

God chose you for a time such as this to show Himself powerful through you. It doesn't matter what people say about you or about your past. God chose to have compassion on you and no one can contest that. God has started something special within you and He will not stop until your story is complete. Thank God for the mercy and the grace we take advantage of daily. He's the reason you're still here with the chance to do things better than you have before. Be grateful that we have such a forgiving God!

Call Out To The Lord

"O LORD my God, I cried out to You for help, And You healed me." Psalm 30:2 (NKJV)

Whenever you are hurting or going through hard times, reach out to God. Ask Him for His help with whatever you are struggling with. God does not abandon His children. If you call out to Him, He will heal you with His mighty power. Before you try other methods to stop hurting, give the Most High a try. He keeps His promises to all His people. Believe wholeheartedly in God and His power to heal you. Once you are healed, go out and tell anyone who will listen how God healed you so they too can witness the power of God. You are not alone. Reach out to Jesus and call on Him anytime. He is the best at healing your heart and meeting your needs.

God Gives Rest To The Weary

"Come to Me, all you who are weary and burdened, and I will give you rest. Take My yoke upon you and learn from Me, for I am gentle and humble in heart, and you will find rest for your souls. For My yoke is easy and My burden is light."
Matthew 11:28-30 (NIV)

If you're tired of living sinfully, Jesus invites you to come to Him. He's ready to help you and teach you how to live righteously. He will hold you in His hand and carry your burdens. He won't force you to do anything. He gives you the choice to come to Him. If you choose Him, you will no longer suffer alone in darkness. He wants to give you light and sight. His way is much easier than living in sin. Satan desires to give you death, but Jesus desires to pour out His love over you and give you abundant life.

Live In Peace With Everyone

———◆———

"Do not repay anyone evil for evil. Be careful to do what is right in the eyes of everyone. If it is possible, as far as it depends on you, live at peace with everyone. Do not take revenge, my dear friends, but leave room for God's wrath, for it is written: 'It is Mine to avenge; I will repay,' says the Lord."
Romans 12:17-19 (NIV)

People are going to hurt you in this world. It may be loved ones or strangers, but don't fall into their trap. Don't allow someone's evil actions to change who the Lord is shaping you to be. You have the Most High on your side. God will avenge you and repay all who does evil to you. It's not your place to repay them for what they've done. God called you to be a peacemaker. Live in peace with everyone, not just those who do good to you.

Put On The Armor Of Light

—◆—

"And do this, understanding the present time: The hour has already come for you to wake up from your slumber, because our salvation is nearer now than when we first believed. The night is nearly over; the day is almost here. So let us put aside the deeds of darkness and put on the armor of light." Romans 13:11-12 (NIV)

Pay attention to what's happening in the world. We are closer to the end times. None of us know the last day we will live on this earth, but it's time to wake up and open your eyes. Since you don't know your last day on earth, work hard everyday to put aside any evilness. Work hard to stop sinning. Live a clean life away from any darkness. Live righteously as you walk with Jesus staying very close to Him. He is teaching you how to live in His light.

The Lord Will Make You Stand

"Who are you to judge someone else's servant? To their own master, servants stand or fall. And they will stand, for the Lord is able to make them stand." Romans 14:4 (NIV)

We are all people just trying to find our way through life. Most people go through a period of time where they're not living in a way pleasing to God. No one is perfect. If you see your brother or sister fall, don't talk bad about them. Pray for them and help them in any way possible. Remember how you felt when you stumbled before you judge anyone else. Give them words to help uplift them and do all you can in your power to show them you care. God is the only One who can judge any of us. If you fall, it's not over. God will strengthen you and stand you back up. He will finish what He started in you!

Delight In The Lord's Law

"Blessed is the one who does not walk in step with the wicked or stand in the way that sinners take or sit in the company of mockers, but whose delight is in the law of the Lord, and who meditates on His law day and night." Psalm 1:1-2 (NIV)

God will reach down right in the middle of sinners and pull you out from among them. When you are blessed with a second chance, don't take it for granted. He saved you out of that dark world so He could strengthen you and teach you His ways. Be open to what God is showing you. He blessed you with eyes to see Him and ears to hear Him. You were chosen to go out and make a difference. He chose you to open the door for others to come in. Be sure to learn His Word daily since God gave you such a great responsibility to lead others.

Do What God Told You To Do

———◆———

"And in fact, you do love all of God's family throughout Macedonia. Yet we urge you, brothers and sisters, to do so more and more, and to make it your ambition to lead a quiet life: You should mind your own business and work with your hands, just as we told you, so that your daily life may win the respect of outsiders and so that you will not be dependent on anybody." 1 Thessalonians 4:10-12 (NIV)

Love others around you, but also stay out of their business unless they ask you for help. If you're busy doing what God called you to do, then you don't have time to stick your nose in other people's business. Live righteously and work hard to do what God called you to do. People will see what you're doing and be inspired to chase their own purpose as they see all you're accomplishing while following Jesus.

Rejoicing Comes In The Morning

"For His anger is but for a moment, His favor is for life; Weeping may endure for a night, but joy comes in the morning."
Psalm 30:5 (NKJV)

It's not pretty when the wrath of God comes upon you, but it's necessary to keep you in line. God won't allow His children to fall into the ways of sinners. God's children can't get away with the same things others get away with because of God's plan for their lives. God disciplines the ones He loves. Although you may experience His anger at times, you're still in good hands because of His favor over you. If you're feeling down at the end of the day after experiencing His anger, don't fall into sadness. The next day is a chance to start over. God's mercies are new every morning. Be grateful for God's love and favor.

AUGUST 10ᵀᴴ

Wisdom Yields Patience

"The discretion of a man makes him slow to anger, And his glory is to overlook a transgression." Proverbs 19:11 (NKJV)

You can't control other people or try to make them the person you think they should be because you're not God. Some people may hurt you intentionally or unintentionally, but it's wise to step back and allow God to avenge you. It takes faith, wisdom, and patience to allow God to handle your situation. It's hard not to get revenge when someone hurts you or offends you, but give it to God. When you let go of your anger and give it to God, it frees you to receive perfect peace. You think more clearly when you are in perfect peace and it strengthens you the more you learn to let God take care of your problems. God will bless you with glory as you allow Him to avenge you.

AUGUST 11ᵀᴴ

Receive The Peace Of Jesus

───❖───

"Peace I leave with you, My peace I give to you; not as the world gives do I give to you. Let not your heart be troubled, neither let it be afraid." John 14:27 (NKJV)

Jesus didn't leave us alone to face the world by ourselves. Those who accept Christ as their Lord and Savior will receive the Holy Spirit. The Holy Spirit molds you, guides you, and teaches you as He leads you through life. Now that you have this Helper, it's easier to have inner peace. Trouble will still rise up in your life, but don't be afraid. You were blessed with a gift from God. God's gift to you is the Holy Spirit. You can remain in perfect peace in the midst of trouble because you know you aren't in this world alone. Pay attention to the signs all around you. God is with you right now. Open your eyes.

Be Careful Not To Isolate

"Two are better than one, because they have a good return for their labor: If either of them falls down, one can help the other up. But pity anyone who falls and has no one to help them up. Also, if two lie down together, they will keep warm. But how can one keep warm alone?" Ecclesiastes 4:9-11 (NIV)

Be grateful if you have a great team around you. Make it known to the people you love that you appreciate them as often as you can. When God blesses you with an opportunity, your team will help you accomplish your mission faster by working together. Eat the fruits of your labor together. Keep a great team around you that you trust will help you back up if you fall and do the same for them. It's harder for Satan to keep you down when you have a great team around you.

God Chooses The Weak

―――◈―――

"Brothers and sisters, think of what you were when you were called. Not many of you were wise by human standards; not many were influential; not many were of noble birth. But God chose the foolish things of the world to shame the wise; God chose the weak things of the world to shame the strong. God chose the lowly things of this world and the despised things— and the things that are not—to nullify the things that are, so that no one may boast before Him." 1 Corinthians 1:26-29 (NIV)

God chose you when you were cast out by everyone. People counted you out and lost all hope for you, but God stepped in to clean you up. He picked you up and transformed your life, but not for you to brag about. God chose you to show Himself strong. He chose you to show His mighty power.

AUGUST 14ᵀᴴ

God's Great Unfailing Love

"For no one is cast off by the Lord forever. Though He brings grief, He will show compassion, so great is His unfailing love."
Lamentations 3:31-32 (NIV)

Following Christ isn't always easy. Sometimes God will test you and you may fail His test. The tests are not designed to trick you or make you stumble, but they are designed to strengthen you for the next level in your life. Things don't get easier when you choose to follow Jesus, but He strengthens you to deal with the difficult circumstances life can bring. If you fail a test, don't get discouraged. God is gracious and merciful. He is compassionate and He will forgive you, but you still have to face the consequences of your actions. Consequences help to teach you and to mold you into the person God created you to be.

Moving On From The Past

―――⟡―――

"Brothers and sisters, I do not consider myself yet to have taken hold of it. But one thing I do: Forgetting what is behind and straining toward what is ahead, I press on toward the goal to win the prize for which God has called me Heavenward in Christ Jesus." Philippians 3:13-14 (NIV)

Trust God fully when He calls you to move to the next level. Learn from your past, but leave it behind you. Once God moves you into better, continue trusting Him to guide you through the uncomfortableness of newness. It's easy to go back to what you're used to because it feels safe, but you can't grow if you remain in your safe place. Stop letting your feelings lead you and allow your faith to lead you. God called you to move forward. Rise up and receive the reward God has for you.

Shine Like The Stars Of Heaven

―◈―

"And they that be wise shall shine as the brightness of the firmament; and they that turn many to righteousness as the stars for ever and ever." Daniel 12:3 (KJV)

Before you were chosen to make a difference here on earth, you did things your own way apart from God. You weren't considered wise apart from the Lord, but now God has chosen to fill you with wisdom and light. God chose you in darkness and gave you light. God will place you wherever He chooses and use you as a vessel to give other dark places light. He gave you a promotion in the Kingdom because He can trust you. Your new job is to lead others to righteousness. He's made you into a bright star here on earth to help light up dark places. Continue on in God's love, peace, wisdom, and power. You are very blessed!

God Is Revealing His Mysteries

"In Him we have redemption through His blood, the forgiveness of sins, in accordance with the riches of God's grace that He lavished on us. With all wisdom and understanding, He made known to us the mystery of His will according to His good pleasure, which He purposed in Christ, to be put into effect when the times reach their fulfillment—to bring unity to all things in Heaven and on earth under Christ." Ephesians 1:7-10 (NIV)

God sent Christ to pay your debt and to forgive you for your sins. He chose to bless you with wisdom and understanding. He's revealing His mysteries to you as you continue following Him. God is teaching you what purpose you serve. God reveals your destiny to you in His perfect timing. He created you to rise up at this time for this very moment. Keep Your eyes on the Lord as He reveals your true calling on this earth.

Guard Your Lips When Speaking

———⊰◈⊱———

"He that keepeth his mouth keepeth his life: but he that openeth wide his lips shall have destruction." Proverbs 13:3 (KJV)

Be careful about the story you tell yourself everyday because you could be destroying your own self by what you repeat over and over to yourself. Be aware of what comes out of your mouth because words have power. If you continue to speak negatively about yourself, you start to actually believe it and become what you feared most. Change the story you tell yourself. Speak positive affirmations over yourself daily. Speak and write down exactly what you want to become every morning. Start your day off with a positive mindset. Eventually, you will see major changes in your life. Notice how powerful the story you tell yourself can physically affect your life.

God will Provide A Way Out

"So, if you think you are standing firm, be careful that you don't fall! No temptation has overtaken you except what is common to mankind. And God is faithful; He will not let you be tempted beyond what you can bear. But when you are tempted, He will also provide a way out so that you can endure it." 1 Corinthians 10:12-13 (NIV)

When God opens a door for you, don't assume nothing can stop you. Be watchful! Satan sits in front of every open door trying to keep you from entering into the next level. Satan can't move without God's permission. If you're being tested, it's because God allowed it to happen in order to strengthen you. You can't move into the next level if you can't handle a bigger devil. When temptation rises up, look for the way out God has provided for you.

The Evil Is Used For God's Good

———◇———

"But Joseph said to them, 'Don't be afraid. Am I in the place of God? You intended to harm me, but God intended it for good to accomplish what is now being done, the saving of many lives.'" Genesis 50:19-20 (NIV)

God uses your enemies to move you into the place He wants you to be. Your enemies came up against you and tried to do you harm, but they were being used by God to move you into a better place. God will always use your enemies to bless you. At first you may not understand why your enemies attacked you, but nothing happens without God allowing it. In hindsight you realize that if it wasn't for your enemies, you wouldn't be standing right in the middle of your blessing. God moved you to a place to bring light to the place. Be grateful and bless your enemies.

Love Your Brothers And Sisters

———◆———

"Whoever claims to love God yet hates a brother or sister is a liar. For whoever does not love their brother and sister, whom they have seen, cannot love God, whom they have not seen."
1 John 4:20 (NIV)

God is love and if you are His you are filled with love. God says that if you keep His commandments then you love Him. One of His commandments is to love others. If Jesus lives within your heart, then you can't hate anyone. If you love God and haven't seen God, then why is it so hard to love the people around you that you can see? If you love others unconditionally, it doesn't mean you won't ever be hurt. Forgive others when they hurt you. Forgiving others makes you whole. You take your power back from whoever hurt you by forgiving them and you remain free from hate.

God will Approve Your Journey

———⬥———

"Then they said to him, 'Please inquire of God to learn whether our journey will be successful.' The priest answered them, 'Go in peace. Your journey has the Lord's approval.'"
Judges 18:5-6 (NIV)

There comes a moment in your life when God blesses you with an opportunity to choose His way or to remain on the same path you're used to. God calls you to certain places He wants you to go, but He won't make you go to those places. If you decide to walk with God, pray to Him before you make a big move. Be sure that you're headed in the right direction. Looking at your journey as a whole can be overwhelming, but always remember that a thousand mile journey starts with a single step. You will accomplish so much more if you move toward your destination one step at a time.

AUGUST 23RD

God Will Bring You Glory

⟩◆⟨

"I consider that our present sufferings are not worth comparing with the glory that will be revealed in us." Romans 8:18 (NIV)

You will still experience hardships as you walk with Christ, but He gives you the tools to overcome these hardships. Everyone has pain, but you can't allow your pain to become permanent. There is always purpose in your pain. Stop wallowing in it and fight. One day you will understand that the suffering you are experiencing will be the very thing that blesses you with glory and power. The pain you suffer at times is temporary. It's a part of the process which brings you into a place of power. Your pain gives you the power to understand how others may be suffering and the power to help them as they struggle with the same battle you've already conquered!

Run On The Heights

"The Sovereign Lord is my strength; He makes my feet like the feet of a deer, He enables me to tread on the heights."
Habakkuk 3:19 (NIV)

You have to become tougher when you are promoted into the next level. Becoming tougher isn't becoming meaner. Becoming tougher means becoming adaptable to whatever circumstances the next level brings your way. As you rise into something new and something foreign, it can be a little uncomfortable. The uncomfortable feeling means you're growing. Once you come into your new level, God will help you adjust and adapt to your new position. He will strengthen you for this new level. Trust Him fully as He promotes you to the next stage. Things around you may not look or feel like you expected, but you will adapt soon. Just don't quit!

Get Ready For God's Increase

"May the Lord, the God of your ancestors, increase you a thousand times and bless you as He has promised!"
Deuteronomy 1:11 (NIV)

God is pouring out His favor over you as He blesses wherever your feet walk. As you're being lifted higher up, the devil is looking for ways to stop you. The bigger the devil, the higher the level. The size of your devil determines the level you're on. If you aren't feeling any pressure while moving forward, it's a sign that you may not be on the level you should be on, which means it's time to step your game up. Stop playing it safe. Go after your calling with everything you got. The higher up you go, the more pressure you experience. Praise God when your devil gets bigger because it's a sign you're rising to an even higher position.

A New Door Has Opened

⟫◆⟪

"But I will stay on at Ephesus until Pentecost, because a great door for effective work has opened to me, and there are many who oppose me." 1 Corinthians 16:8-9 (NIV)

God is opening doors for you to enter into. He is making a way for you to accomplish your mission. Don't hesitate to walk through any door that God opens for you. He is walking through the door with you. When you decide to get up and go after your calling, there are going to be people that Satan puts in place to distract you from your destination. You have to remain focused on your goal. If someone hates you for no reason, it's a sign that you're closer to your destination. Satan plays dirty. He sends haters to make you doubt everything God put within you, but don't get discouraged. Soar even higher!

God Called You to Be A Leader

———❖———

"But now thy kingdom shall not continue: the Lord hath sought Him a man after His own heart, and the Lord hath commanded him to be captain over His people, because thou hast not kept that which the Lord commanded thee." 1 Samuel 13:14 (KJV)

God moves people out of certain positions so He can put His people in position. God chooses people after His own heart to be leaders. He chose you for a specific purpose because of your passion. It takes time for God to prepare you for the new position He has for you. He is equipping your mind with knowledge and wisdom to match the passion already within your heart for the position He has waiting just ahead of you. Don't get tired of doing everything He asks you to do because your opportunity is closer than you realize.

AUGUST 28TH

Forgive And Comfort Others

⟹◆⟸

"Now instead, you ought to forgive and comfort him, so that he will not be overwhelmed by excessive sorrow. I urge you, therefore, to reaffirm your love for him." 2 Corinthians 2:7-8 (NIV)

Satan is looking for any kind of opening he can come through to tear you away from your family. He knows that if he can get you alone, he can play with your mind. If you isolate yourself from your loved ones, the enemy will attack you by putting negative thoughts in your head causing anger or depression. Stay close to your positive friends and family because Satan can't overpower a whole army of God's children. Your real friends and family will uplift you when you aren't feeling too sure about yourself. Stay connected to God and positive people. If someone hurts you, forgive them.

God Is Sending You Out

"Again Jesus said, 'Peace be with you! As the Father has sent Me, I am sending you.'" John 20:21 (NIV)

You were chosen by God for a time such as this to accomplish a great mission. Before God brings you into position, you will be tested. Can you praise God when everything isn't going your way? Will you stay committed to Him? God will move you up in position based on your heart. Don't focus on the position, but focus on the mission and God will exalt you. God will change your position to accomplish your mission. Sometimes God will use someone in a lower position to bless you so be careful for how you treat everyone. You never know who is holding the key to the door that opens up to the next level. Idle time is your enemy when you're on a mission so keep moving forward.

You Are Being Transformed

—◆—

"Now the Lord is that Spirit: and where the Spirit of the Lord is, there is liberty. But we all, with open face beholding as in a glass the glory of the Lord, are changed into the same image from glory to glory, even as by the Spirit of the Lord."
2 Corinthians 3:17-18 (KJV)

Begin each morning with God. Before you walk out your door, take time to quiet your mind and pray to Him. If you start your day with Him, you will walk in freedom. As God moves you up a level, He is filling you with power and strength. Everyday you're being changed little by little. There will be many blessings along the way, but there will also be challenges in between those blessings. Don't be discouraged because the challenges make you stronger as you are transformed into a person filled with God's power.

AUGUST 31ST

Your Heavenly Dwelling

———◆◆◆———

"For while we are in this tent, we groan and are burdened, because we do not wish to be unclothed but to be clothed instead with our Heavenly dwelling, so that what is mortal may be swallowed up by life. Now the One who has fashioned us for this very purpose is God, who has given us the Spirit as a deposit, guaranteeing what is to come." 2 Corinthians 5:4-5 (NIV)

This physical world is the temporary womb God is using to develop your spirit for eternity with Him. Once you are fully developed by God and your story here is finished, your spirit moves on into the spiritual realm. Change your perspective on the way you experience your life in this world since you know your life on earth is just the preparation stage for the spiritual realm which will be forever. Enjoy life!

SEPTEMBER 1ST

Trust God's Way Fully

"Where were you when I laid the earth's foundation? Tell me, if you understand. Who marked off its dimensions? Surely you know! Who Stretched a measuring line across it." Job 38:4-5 (NIV)

Job in the bible was upset with God because of all that he lost and he questioned God. He couldn't understand why God allowed him to suffer like this even though he was faithful to Him. At the end of the story, Job was blessed with double for his trouble. When things aren't going the way you've expected, it's hard not to question God. You won't always understand the point of the pain you're experiencing, but trust that God has a reason for all your pain. Although it hurts, remain faithful to God through it all. He will bless you for your faithfulness in the good times and the harder times. You will find purpose in your pain.

God Will Make Your Name Great

―――◆―――

"I will make you into a great nation, and I will bless you; I will make your name great, and you will be a blessing. I will bless those who bless you, and whoever curses you I will curse; and all peoples on earth will be blessed through you." Genesis 12:2-3 (NIV)

God called you into His light. He is transforming you into a person of power. He is using you to do great things, but stay focused. The enemy will use people to distract you or throw you off balance, especially when you're closer to your destination. God will continue to prosper you as He pours out His favor over you. There will be people who hate you for no reason because of how blessed you are. They will try to curse you, but God will curse them. Be grateful for God's protection and His favor over you.

SEPTEMBER 3RD

Take Time To Rest

———✦———

"For in six days the Lord made the Heavens and the earth, the sea, and all that is in them, but He rested on the seventh day. Therefore the Lord blessed the Sabbath day and made it holy." Exodus 20:11 (NIV)

There is a lot of pressure in being the person you were created to be, but you must also enjoy the journey as you are becoming that person. Enjoying the journey as you get closer to your destination is the key to being truly happy. You need to have a balance between work and play. Even God rested in between His work and enjoyed the fruits of His labor. As you work hard to reach your destination, add some positive play time along the way. This is how you enjoy your journey toward greatness and how you avoid getting stressed out as you move up another level.

SEPTEMBER 4TH

Only A Few Find The Way

"Enter through the narrow gate. For wide is the gate and broad is the road that leads to destruction, and many enter through it. But small is the gate and narrow the road that leads to life, and only a few find it." Matthew 7:13-14 (NIV)

The greatest thing God gives to us is the power to choose. Be careful not to choose things based off of the pain you're feeling in the present moment. Make a choice that serves a greater vision. Don't miss your moment to choose something greater that can help change the trajectory of the generations coming after you. The choice you make today will affect your children and their children. When you choose to take the road that leads to life, it gets difficult. Remain strong in your spirit and trust God to be with you to guide you on your journey.

The Lord Will Shape You

———◆———

"But the pot he was shaping from the clay was marred in his hands; so the potter formed it into another pot, shaping it as seemed best to him." Jeremiah 18:4 (NIV)

God is the Potter and you're the clay. He is shaping you into something beautiful. Although the process can be painful, remain grateful. God puts you through the process before He blesses you with the promise. The process is what fills you with strength to handle the success waiting ahead of you. Anything you get too fast, you will also lose fast. Thank God for strengthening you through the process as He prepares you for the promise. Once you reach your promise, you receive power through God. The test is not what you do when you're weak without power, but the real test is what you do when you're in power.

Jesus Is The Head Cornerstone

———◆———

"The stone which the builders refused is become the head stone of the corner." Psalm 118:22 (KJV)

When everyone else stepped over you and rejected you, God picked you up to use you for something great. God chose you when everyone else doubted you. The one who is overlooked and cast out is usually the one God chooses to use for great exploits. Jesus was also rejected, but He is who holds us up to keep us from falling. Your second half of your life won't look like the first half. You have come to a point in your life where things are changing for the better. You still have to fight for your blessings, but they are yours. A good fight is healthy for you and keeps you full of God's purpose. A good fight keeps you full of life so continue to fight until your last breath.

SEPTEMBER 7TH

Jesus Suffered For You

———◆———

"Now My soul is troubled, and what shall I say? 'Father, save Me from this hour?' But for this purpose I came to this hour." John 12:27 (NKJV)

Jesus was tortured right before He was persecuted. It was necessary for Him to die so you could live. He gave Himself to death so He could take the power away from Satan who fights constantly to conquer your soul. We too must suffer with Christ so we can also be glorified with Christ. Suffering is not the end, but it's the beginning of new life. God will give new life to those who are able to withstand the attacks of the enemy. You may be going through a tough time right now, but keep your eyes focused on the prize ahead of you. Suffering strengthens you for the position God has waiting for you. Keep moving forward.

Peace Be With You

———◆———

"Finally, brothers and sisters, rejoice! Strive for full restoration, encourage one another, be of one mind, live in peace. And the God of love and peace will be with you." 2 Corinthians 13:11 (NIV)

God chose to give you life and to restore you. After you are strengthened, God uses you as a vessel to spread His message. He uses you to strengthen and encourage others who come into your life. Learn God's Word to receive wisdom and knowledge. Ask God for understanding as you study His Word. As you are filled with His Word, you go through a transformation. As you remain in Christ, you realize that your suffering is what is strengthening you for God's promise. God is with you through every step filling you with His love, peace, and power to do all He's calling you to do.

SEPTEMBER 9TH

The Importance Of Rest

———⋘◆⋙———

"Six days thou shalt work, but on the seventh day thou shalt rest: in earing and in harvest thou shalt rest." Exodus 34:21 (KJV)

God created you to be a hardworking warrior in His Kingdom. It's important to work hard when God opens a new door for you to walk through. Satan will use anything he can to throw you off balance as you reach the next level. Satan will find ways to keep you so busy that you wear yourself out to the point of crashing. God wants you to work hard, but He also wants you to take time to rest. Take time to rejuvenate yourself and to re-energize your spirit. You are no good to the Kingdom and to people if you are too tired to give them all of you. Rest up, enjoy some "you time", and then go back out to join the fight with God's people.

You Will Overcome The Enemy

"You, dear children, are from God and have overcome them, because the One who is in you is greater than the one who is in the world." 1 John 4:4 (NIV)

Do not doubt your power to make an impact. God brought you out of captivity from Satan's grip to use you in a mighty way. God put you here on earth to make a difference in the world. You have a purpose within you that is waiting to be discovered. The closer you get to discovering your purpose, the harder Satan will fight you. When you are being fought by Satan, don't get discouraged. Always remember that God is all powerful and He lives within you. This means that you are stronger than any devil that comes against you. You are more powerful than you realize. Use the power God has given you to reach your destination.

SEPTEMBER 11TH

God Blesses Hard Work

———◆———

"Whatever you do, work at it with all your heart, as working for the Lord, not for human masters, since you know that you will receive an inheritance from the Lord as a reward. It is the Lord Christ you are serving." Colossians 3:23-24 (NIV)

God gave you a mission down here on earth. He blessed you with life so He could use you to reach out and help others. What is your calling? What is your true purpose here on earth? Once you come into alignment with God's plan for your life, work hard to please Him. You are doing God's work so be sure to put a 100% into everything He leads you to do. As you open your heart to God's plan, He will bless all that your hands touch and wherever your feet walk. Remember that your reward will come from God in the end and not from people.

SEPTEMBER 12ᵀᴴ

You Are A New Person

"I have been crucified with Christ and I no longer live, but Christ lives in me. The life I now live in the body, I live by faith in the Son of God, who loved me and gave Himself for me." Galatians 2:20 (NIV)

You have to be crucified with Christ before He can transform you into a new person. Your old ways have to be put away before God can use you. As you walk with God, He will change the way you speak, the way you understand, and the way you think. You can't expect to receive God's promises if you are still living in your old ways. God will promote you when you allow Him to transform you completely. As you reach for your new life, allow your old way of thinking to fade away. Gain a new perspective on the way you see things and watch your life change for the better.

SEPTEMBER 13TH

Blessings And Prosperity

"When you eat the labor of your hands, You shall be happy and it shall be well with you." Psalm 128:2 (NKJV)

Sometimes people think that once they come to God everything will be magically fixed and everything they do will be easy. They think blessings will just fall into their laps. God does bless His children, but you still have to work for your blessings. The difference between being a child of God is that He will fill you with His strength and power to do what He's called you to do. God will open doors for you, but the enemy will sit in front of every open door to do all he can to stop you. As you labor for God, He will reward you with prosperity. He will pour you out a blessing you don't have room enough to receive. Work hard and get ready to receive a great harvest.

Labor For Your Food

"For even when we were with you, we gave you this rule: 'The one who is unwilling to work shall not eat.'" 2 Thessalonians 3:10 (NIV)

When God brings you out of darkness, He strengthens you through His Holy Spirit. He blesses you with wisdom, strength, and power to go after your calling. When God opens a new door for you, run through it without stopping. The moment you allow yourself to become stagnant, everything God is trying to give you will come to a halt. Anyone who refuses to work refuses to be blessed. God will bless whatever you "DO". If you refuse to do anything, there is nothing for God to bless. Get up, go out, and work hard for the Lord so He can bless you with overflow. God loves to bless His children, but He teaches us to work for our blessings as well.

SEPTEMBER 15TH

Christ Set You Free

⟨⟩

"It is for freedom that Christ has set us free. Stand firm, then, and do not let yourselves be burdened again by a yoke of slavery." Galatians 5:1 (NIV)

You have been set free by our Heavenly Father. You were dead in your spirit before you gave your life to Christ, but now you are alive in Him. You're no longer a slave to your flesh and to the world. You walk in complete freedom as you are led by the Holy Spirit. Now that you are free, be careful not to allow yourself to be enslaved by the enemy. Satan will do all he can to set traps for your feet and to bring you back into bondage. Always remember the pain you felt when you were chasing after the things of this world. You can remain free and in perfect peace if you stand strong against the temptations of this world.

Refresh Others To Be Refreshed

———◆———

"A generous person will prosper; whoever refreshes others will be refreshed." Proverbs 11:25 (NIV)

It's very important to treat others with respect and kindness. If you see your brother or sister down and out, be an ear for them when they need to talk. Find out what you can do to help them. Do whatever is in your power to do in order to keep them lifted up. You will receive back whatever you give out. If you want God to pour out His favor over you, be willing to use your favor to help others. Continue to provide for others, love others, and pray with others when they are in need. God will fill you up and prosper you if He can trust you to help others when they're struggling. Allow God's love and goodness to overflow through you into the lives of those around you.

SEPTEMBER 17TH

A Wise Tongue Heals

"The words of the reckless pierce like swords, but the tongue of the wise brings healing." Proverbs 12:18 (NIV)

Be careful of the things you say to people. Your words have the power to either hurt people or to heal people. Your words have the power to end someone's life or to give someone life. It's important to watch what you say to other people because once you say certain words, you can never take the words back. If you are angry with someone, take time to think and pray about the situation. Before you approach the person you're upset with, be sure to give yourself and the other person time to calm down. You never know the damage your words can cause to someone's spirit until it's too late. Ask God to give you the right words when you feel the time is right.

Keep Yourself Filled Up

⟫◈⟪

"But Jesus said, 'Someone touched Me; I know that power has gone out from Me.'" Luke 8:46 (NIV)

While Jesus was walking a woman touched Him so she could be healed. When she touched Him, Jesus could feel the power leave Him. When everyone is pulling at you for help, it can become exhausting. You can't allow yourself to give all you have to the point that you become tired and empty yourself. Take time to fill yourself back up or you won't be any good to anyone else. Your own peace and sanity needs to come first. Don't allow anyone to draw everything from you leaving you with nothing. Put your own mental health and your own needs first, then you can be an even better help to your loved ones. Everyone won't be understanding, but the ones who really love you will get it.

Trials Produce Perseverance

—◆—

"Consider it pure joy, my brothers and sisters, whenever you face trials of many kinds, because you know that the testing of your faith produces perseverance. Let perseverance finish its work so that you may be mature and complete, not lacking anything." James 1:2-4 (NIV)

Learn to overcome anger and bitterness. The enemy sets traps for your feet which causes bitterness. Staying bitter takes away your freedom to think your greatest thoughts. You need your freedom to think your best thoughts when you go on conquests. Conquests are what keep you going strong and full a life. Decide in your heart and mind that you're a champion, not just a conqueror. A conqueror is defined by the fight you fought, but a champion is defined by the winner you are.

Chosen For Greatness

———◆———

"As a prisoner for the Lord, then, I urge you to live a life worthy of the calling you have received. Be completely humble and gentle; be patient, bearing with one another in love. Make every effort to keep the unity of the Spirit through the bond of peace. There is one body and one Spirit, just as you were called to one hope when you were called; one Lord, one faith, one baptism; one God and Father of all, who is over all and through all and in all." Ephesians 4:1-6 (NIV)

God created you for greatness! As He draws out the gifts He's placed within you, remain humble as He lifts you up. Run through the door God opened for you. Use your gifts to inspire others. You have God's Spirit living within, which means you already have all you need to take hold of your destiny. Run after it!

SEPTEMBER 21ST

Make The Most Of Life

"This is why it is said: "Wake up, sleeper, rise from the dead, and Christ will shine on you." Be very careful, then, how you live—not as unwise but as wise, making the most of every opportunity, because the days are evil." Ephesians 5:14-16 (NIV)

God meets you in your darkest place to wake you from your slumber. He fills you with light, so you can be a light for others. Stay alert because Satan is very crafty. Satan sits in front of every open door trying to keep you from entering in. He can't close the door so he plays every trick he can to keep you from entering into the door. Praise God whenever you're under attack because it means God has opened the door to the next level. Take hold of the opportunity God has blessed you with to bring light into this dark world.

Ask, Believe, Receive

❖

"Therefore I tell you, whatever you ask for in prayer, believe that you have received it, and it will be yours." Mark 11:24 (NIV)

God moves at the sound of your voice. If you remain silent, you won't receive anything. Satan tries to keep you so stressed out that you stop asking for anything. Don't be silenced. Ask God for your heart's desires and He will bless you. Don't worry about what others say as you go after your purpose. You won't be defeated by what people say about you. You will only be defeated by what you say about you. When you believe wholeheartedly in your purpose, God will lift you up. Be willing to invest your time and money into your own cause, then others will be willing to invest as well. If you sacrifice all you have, God will bless your sacrifice.

SEPTEMBER 23RD

Do Not Worry About Tomorrow

"Therefore do not worry about tomorrow, for tomorrow will worry about itself. Each day has enough trouble of its own."
Matthew 6:34 (NIV)

It's important to live in the now. Don't allow your worry for the future to take your peace and joy for today. If you're worrying about the future, you can't think your best thoughts. You can't think clear thoughts which will shape your future. Be present in every moment. Allow yourself to experience the goodness and fullness of life. As human beings, we tend to make things bigger in our minds than they really are. God already has the thing you are most worried about taken care of. Continue to trust in the power of God as you walk hand in hand with Him. Enjoy this day as you walk in freedom knowing that God has it already worked out.

All Things Are Working Together

"And we know that in all things God works for the good of those who love Him, who have been called according to His purpose." Romans 8:28 (NIV)

God put you on this earth to make a difference. He gave you gifts to encourage and inspire others. There is something unique about you. God put something within you that no one else has. Figure out what that something is and use it to uplift others. It's a blessing to see your gifts make a difference in the lives of others, but it won't always feel like a blessing. The enemy attacks you more when you're gifted because he knows your gifts bring freedom to the lives of others, giving them light. This is why your passion has to be strong as you go after your purpose because your pain will make you want to quit, but keep it moving.

No One Can Shut The Open Door

"I know your deeds. See, I have placed before you an open door that no one can shut. I know that you have little strength, yet you have kept My word and have not denied My name."
Revelation 3:8 (NIV)

God knows the time you put in to do His work. He will bless every sacrifice you make for His Kingdom. God is opening doors for you that no one can close. Don't allow fear of what others think or say stop you from speaking the name of Jesus everywhere you go. God has a hedge of protection around you. As you do God's work, He will protect you and provide for you. He takes great care of His children. Once God reveals Himself to you, no one can make you doubt Him. Walk with God through the open doors. He will refresh your spirit and renew your strength as you do His work.

Remain Humble In All Things

———⊰◈⊱———

"In your relationships with one another, have the same mindset as Christ Jesus: Who, being in very nature God, did not consider equality with God something to be used to His own advantage; rather, He made Himself nothing by taking the very nature of a servant, being made in human likeness. And being found in appearance as a man, He humbled Himself by becoming obedient to death—even death on a cross!"
Philippians 2:5-8 (NIV)

Jesus was exalted to His highest place. Although He is a King, He remained humble. He didn't abuse His power. Be like Christ when God promotes you. Remember that it's only through God's power that you're being promoted to greatness. Once you reach the next level, remain grateful because your gratitude and humility is what will activate God's power.

The Lord Will Fight For You

"Moses answered the people, 'Do not be afraid. Stand firm and you will see the deliverance the Lord will bring you today. The Egyptians you see today you will never see again. The Lord will fight for you; you need only to be still.'" Exodus 14:13-14 (NIV)

When your past is threatening to take you back to where you used to be, DON'T BE AFRAID. Trust fully in the power of God. He didn't save you only to leave you now. Walk in perfect peace knowing that God is your Father and there is nothing too hard for Him. Believe in God's power and pray to our Heavenly Father because the prayers of the righteous doesn't go unheard. When the enemy rises against you, be still, stand firm and allow God to fight for you. He will defeat your enemies and you will never see them again.

Secret Of Being Content

"I know what it is to be in need, and I know what it is to have plenty. I have learned the secret of being content in any and every situation, whether well fed or hungry, whether living in plenty or in want. I can do all this through Him who gives me strength. Philippians 4:12-13 (NIV)

It's important to learn how to survive in lack and abundance. Everyone has times in their life when they feel like they're on a roller coaster. One minute you're up feeling like you're on top of the world and then the next minute you're not sure you're going to make it. The more anointed you are, the more the enemy attacks you. Before you go to the next level, there is always an attack first. The ones who remain strong through Christ are the ones who will be promoted to the next level.

Glory In Your Suffering

"Not only so, but we also glory in our sufferings, because we know that suffering produces perseverance; perseverance, character; and character, hope. And hope does not put us to shame, because God's love has been poured out into our hearts through the Holy Spirit, who has been given to us." Romans 5:3-5 (NIV)

Suffering is inescapable, but it's all in how you look at your suffering which makes the difference. Change your perspective. Look at problems as opportunities. For example, God allows people to see your struggle and to speak negatively about you so that when He turns your situation around, they will see His power. God is taking you from survival to success. The pain you're experiencing is the platform to your promise. Yesterday is not yours to recover, but tomorrow is yours to win.

Forgive Others Who Repent

―――◆―――

"So watch yourselves. 'If your brother or sister sins against you, rebuke them; and if they repent, forgive them. Even if they sin against you seven times in a day and seven times come back to you saying 'I repent,' you must forgive them.'" Luke 17:3-4 (NIV)

It's hard to stay happy if you're easily offended all the time. The next time you're offended by someone, don't hold a grudge. Satan will use any tactic to tear relationships apart. Satan hates unity. Your unwillingness to forgive others will only make you a prisoner to yourself. Forgiveness is the key to that prison. Forgive the person who hurt you and DROP IT! Don't allow offenses to build a fence between you and your loved ones. If God dropped all of your charges, then why can't you drop someone else's charges?

OCTOBER 1ˢᵀ

I Will Rise

———◆———

"Do not gloat over me, my enemy! Though I have fallen, I will rise. Though I sit in darkness, the Lord will be my light."
Micah 7:8 (NIV)

Some of your choices, good or bad, brought you to the place you're in now. Although there are things that happen in life that you can't control, you have free will to choose to react or respond to whatever happens. Your choice to react in a bad manner will take you into dark places, but your choice to respond in a good manner will bless you with strength and wisdom. Your pain can bring you into a dark depression or your pain can give you power to help strengthen and educate others. Choose to grow from your painful experiences so you can help free others from their chains. Your life begins when you find out who you truly are. You are a warrior!

OCTOBER 2ND

Love Your Enemies

———◆———

"But love your enemies, do good to them, and lend to them without expecting to get anything back. Then your reward will be great, and you will be children of the Most High, because He is kind to the ungrateful and wicked." Luke 6:35 (NIV)

It's hard to love people who intentionally hurt you, but the love of Christ within you overpowers any spirits of evil. The next time your enemy does something hateful, overpower their hate with love. Your enemies will eventually back off of you when they realize your love for them outweighs their hate for you. The love of Christ within you is strong enough to transform your enemy into a follower of Christ. God sees everything you do and He will reward you for showing kindness to your enemies. Love your enemies just as God taught you.

OCTOBER 3RD

God Is With You Always

———◆———

"Have I not commanded you? Be strong and of good courage; do not be afraid, nor be dismayed, for the Lord your God is with you wherever you go." Joshua 1:9 (NKJV)

God will allow you to be unstable when you're in transition to teach you how to activate your core strength and power. Going to another level in your life can feel scary because you don't know how things will turn out. When you're in an unstable position, your instability teaches you how to depend on God in everything. The pressure you feel when problems arise is the very thing that will produce power within you. Your struggles are what makes you truly cry out to God and teaches you how to pray genuine prayers to Him. Once you see God's power working in your life, you will know how real He is and you will never see life the same way again.

OCTOBER 4TH

God Set You Free

"Stand fast therefore in the liberty by which Christ has made us free, and do not be entangled again with a yoke of bondage."
Galatians 5:1 (NKJV)

God chose to free you out of bondage so He could use you in mighty ways. Now that you're free, keep moving forward. The enemy is very cunning. He sets traps for your feet to trip you up. Don't allow yourself to be enslaved again by sin now that God has set you free. Before you make life-changing decisions, ask God for His guidance and His will to be done. You've been chosen by God out of many. Don't ever look back. Once you're chosen, you still go through a process before you come into your purpose. It's important to have a great focus in your life, while maintaining a healthy balance between good clean fun and work.

Your Enemies Will Lose

"And the Lord said to Joshua, 'Do not fear them; for I have delivered them into your hand; not a man of them shall stand before you.'" Joshua 10:8 (NKJV)

God gave you the spirit of a mighty warrior. Everything that has happened in your life up until this point was meant to strengthen you for this very moment. You are filled with the strength and power of God. If anyone rises up to fight you, they will lose and you will win the victory. The battle is not yours, it's the Lord's. God has already won the battle for you. Your only job is to trust God and His Word. He will fight for you and through you. Remain in perfect peace because God fulfills His promises to His children. God can't lie and He promised to deliver your adversaries into your hand, so get ready for victory!

Brothers Or Sisters Stick By You

—◆—

"A friend loveth at all times, and a brother is born for adversity."
Proverbs 17:17 (KJV)

When God blesses you with good people in your life, cherish and love them. Everyone isn't blessed with great friends. You will know when you've found a great friend because they're the ones who stick close to you when trouble arises. Your great friends become like brothers or sisters in your life when trials come to test you. They will be by your side to help strengthen and encourage you when life throws you a curveball. Never take these people for granted. Never take advantage of their kindness. Show your appreciation for them and be forever grateful for them. No one is promised tomorrow so let your brothers and sisters know how much you love them every chance you get.

Avoid The Path Of The Wicked

"Do not set foot on the path of the wicked or walk in the way of evildoers. Avoid it, do not travel on it; turn from it and go on your way. For they cannot rest until they do evil; they are robbed of sleep till they make someone stumble. Proverbs 4:14-16 (NIV)

God sends people into your life to inspire you and strengthen you on your journey, but Satan also sends people to trip you up. Be careful who you allow to have access to you. There are people out there who want nothing more than to see you fall flat on your face and they won't rest until you do. Use discernment and listen to what God is putting within your heart. If someone is becoming more of an issue in your life, ask God for His guidance. Anyone can say they care, but what are their actions saying?

Don't Live Separately From God

"So I tell you this, and insist on it in the Lord, that you must no longer live as the Gentiles do, in the futility of their thinking. They are darkened in their understanding and separated from the life of God because of the ignorance that is in them due to the hardening of their hearts. Having lost all sensitivity, they have given themselves over to sensuality so as to indulge in every kind of impurity, and they are full of greed." Ephesians 4:17-19 (NIV)

When you give your life to Christ, everything won't magically be fixed. Once you make the choice to follow God, He will mold you before He uses you for a higher purpose. Be willing to let things go in order to become the person God meant for you to be. Once He removes the impurities from you, then He will use you.

You Are God's Anointed

—◆—

"As for you, the anointing you received from Him remains in you, and you do not need anyone to teach you. But as His anointing teaches you about all things and as that anointing is real, not counterfeit—just as it has taught you, remain in Him." 1 John 2:27 (NIV)

God has anointed you. God chose you to teach and encourage others. You have been chosen for something great. God has His hand on you and He remains with you as He lights the way for you. It feels awkward at times when you're around others because you have been chosen and set apart. What others call weird, God calls unique. You aren't like anyone else because of the calling on your life. He is walking with you, so there is no reason to be afraid. Remain close to God as He does amazing things through you.

OCTOBER 10TH

The Lord Is Merciful

———◆———

"It is of the Lord's mercies that we are not consumed, because His compassions fail not. They are new every morning: great is thy faithfulness." Lamentations 3:22-23 (KJV)

Life can get difficult and some days you may feel like you're losing your grip, but God pours out His mercy over His children. God knows your heart and your true intentions. He will not allow you to be swallowed up by life if you repent and change the way you are living. If you stumble, God will have compassion on you as He continues to shape you into who you were meant to be. If you stumble, ask God for forgiveness, get back up, and continue to move forward. Every morning is a new day and a new chance to start all over again. Learn from yesterday and do things different. Do things even better today.

What Do You Treasure?

———⟡———

"For where your treasure is, there your heart will be also."
Luke 12:34 (NKJV)

God loves to bless His children abundantly. He pours out His favor over the righteous. As God blesses you, be sure to keep your eyes focused on Him. Don't allow yourself to become focused on the gifts, but instead focus on the Giver. Don't be deceived by the treasures that come when you discover your purpose. Always remember that it was your focus on God that got you where you are in the first place. Whenever you value the gifts more than the Giver, the enemy will lead you astray. If you chase after the treasure and not after the Giver, you will soon fall into the enemy's trap. You will eventually lose it all anyway. Remain focused on God and remain grateful as you humbly follow His lead.

OCTOBER 12ᵀᴴ

Lead A Quiet Life

———◆———

"And in fact, you do love all of God's family throughout Macedonia. Yet we urge you, brothers and sisters, to do so more and more, and to make it your ambition to lead a quiet life: You should mind your own business and work with your hands, just as we told you, so that your daily life may win the respect of outsiders and so that you will not be dependent on anybody." 1 Thessalonians 4:10-12 (NIV)

God raised you up for a time such as this to be a great leader. Love all of God's people and work hard in your God-given purpose. Walk in peace as you focus on all the Lord has called you to do. Mind your own business and lead with action, not only with words. When God blesses you with great gifts, you don't have to promote yourself. Allow your work to speak for itself.

Repent And Believe

"The time has come," He said. "The kingdom of God has come near. Repent and believe the good news!" Mark 1:15 (NIV)

No one knows the exact hour Jesus is coming back, but looking at all that is going on in the world today, we don't seem to have too much time left to get it right. Fill yourself with God's Word daily and allow it to transform you. Everything won't suddenly change the moment you give your life to Christ because it's a process. Nothing great just happens overnight. You have to want change and be willing to go through the necessary process to see your life improve. There may be things that trip you up on your journey, but be sure to get back up stronger than you were before. Continue to fight hard so that when Christ returns, He will find you blameless.

OCTOBER 14TH

God Set You Apart

———◆———

"Before I formed you in the womb I knew you; Before you were born I sanctified you; I ordained you a prophet to the nations." Jeremiah 1:5 (NKJV)

God knew you before the beginning of time. He put you on this earth to accomplish something great. You are God's child, which is why you're able to hear His call. God's children know when they've been called for a great mission. When God calls you something, it doesn't matter what other people call you. That's why God will find you in the middle of sin, bring you out, and clean you up so He can use you. Don't allow people to trap you in how they met you. Continue growing into who you were created to be. Don't allow anyone to stop your mission. Life doesn't begin when you're born, life begins when you find out who you are!

OCTOBER 15TH

Continue Walking Forward

"Brothers and sisters, I do not consider myself yet to have taken hold of it. But one thing I do: Forgetting what is behind and straining toward what is ahead, I press on toward the goal to win the prize for which God has called me heavenward in Christ Jesus." Philippians 3:13-14 (NIV)

God called you to accomplish greatness. Keep walking and don't hesitate. God will provide all you need everytime you take another step. The things you need most in order to make your dream a reality is faith and consistency. Unbecome the person you were before to become the person you were created to be. If you fall, get back up and try again. Once you reach your destination, don't stop there. The destination is your transportation to the next level. Never stop reaching for the prize!

OCTOBER 16TH

Be Careful Not To Judge Others

—————◆—————

"Do not judge, or you too will be judged. For in the same way you judge others, you will be judged, and with the measure you use, it will be measured to you." Matthew 7:1-2 (NIV)

Be careful not to judge others without truly knowing their heart. People who appear good may be living a private sinful life and good people who appear bad may have made mistakes, but need a little guidance to help them find their way. When you judge others, it pushes them further away. Jesus didn't teach us to judge others, but to love others. Live love-conscious, not sin-conscious. People respond better when they're loved. Spread God's Word and allow the power of it to transform people. You have a responsibility to plant seeds, but God will do the growing and changing of that person's heart.

Whatever You Do Will Prosper

———◆———

"That person is like a tree planted by streams of water, which yields its fruit in season and whose leaf does not wither— whatever they do prospers." Psalm 1:3 (NIV)

God fills you with nutrients that make you grow spiritually as you learn His Word. His Word strengthens you for your calling. His Word teaches you to stand firm. Be strengthened and encouraged through God's Word. Refuse the discouraging words that come from people. You are who God says you are. He has the final say in your life. God is pouring out His favor over you and in the right season, if you don't quit, He will prosper you. As you learn to trust His timing and His method, you will come into your purpose. As you're coming into your purpose, you will produce good fruit. Stand firm and trust the process.

OCTOBER 18ᵀᴴ

Work And You Shall Eat

"For even when we were with you, we gave you this rule: 'The one who is unwilling to work shall not eat.'" 2 Thessalonians 3:10 (NIV)

God put gifts within every single one of us. It's important to find out what your gifts are and to use them to inspire, encourage, strengthen, and uplift others. God said He will bless whatever you do. If you do nothing, there is nothing for God to bless. God blesses your sacrifices. Work hard in whatever it is God has called you to do and He will exalt you. God will reward you for the sacrifices you've made for His Kingdom as you run after your purpose. He will pour out His favor and abundance over you as He blesses whatever your hands touch. Enjoy the fruits of your labor after you put in the hard work it takes to pull in the harvest.

A Door Has Opened To You

"But I will stay on at Ephesus until Pentecost, because a great door for effective work has opened to me, and there are many who oppose me." 1 Corinthians 16:8-9 (NIV)

God knows your sacrifices and He will bless you. Stand firm on this level and God will open the door to the next level. Once the door opens, you still have to fight to enter into the door. There is always a devil standing in front of the open door trying to keep you from entering. At first you will feel discouraged because change is uncomfortable, but God closed a door that is no longer useful to you. He has now opened a new door to the next level and a new opportunity. Don't get discouraged when doors close. Look for the door God has opened up for you and thank Him for the open door as you run through it.

OCTOBER 20TH

God Is Your Fortress

"Deliver me from mine enemies, O God: defend me from them that rise up against me." Psalm 59:1 (KJV)

The closer you are to promotion, the more attack you experience. Before every promotion, you are attacked by the enemy. Stand firm and praise God for the next level. God is your protector and He will surround every enemy that is surrounding you. There is no reason to be afraid. God is getting ready to blow through all of your enemies like a mighty rushing wind and He is going to give you the victory over them all. The attack you are experiencing right now is from the enemy who sits in front of the open door. Whenever you are being attacked, praise and thank God since you know this is a sign that God has already opened up the door to the next level for you.

OCTOBER 21ST

Gifts From Above

———◆———

"Every good and perfect gift is from above, coming down from the Father of the Heavenly lights, who does not change like shifting shadows." James 1:17 (NIV)

God put certain gifts within each and every one of us. As you follow Christ, those gifts are revealed. As you grow closer to Jesus, He will draw out the gifts He put within you. God has given you these gifts to use them for His glory. Your gifts are to inspire, encourage, uplift, teach, and strengthen others. Use your gifts to build one another up. God will bless you with more power to do all He's called you to do through your gifts. Your gifts come from up above and cannot be taken from you. God created you with uniqueness. There is no one in the world like you. Use your unique gifts to inspire those around you.

OCTOBER 22ND

You Will Be In Paradise One Day

━━━◆━━━

"Then he said, 'Jesus, remember me when You come into Your Kingdom.' Jesus answered him, 'Truly I tell you, today you will be with Me in paradise.'" Luke 23:42-43 (NIV)

There was a thief on the cross next to Jesus that was being executed for his crime. He asked Jesus to remember him when He came into His Kingdom. Jesus told the thief he would be in paradise with Him. It's never too late to repent no matter how bad your sins may seem. Jesus will forgive you if you repent and ask for forgiveness. You don't have to stay lost. Don't allow the devil to deceive you. It's never too late to receive salvation. You can have one minute left to receive Jesus and He will save you. Give yourself to Christ before it's too late. You never know when you will breathe your last breath.

A Witness Of The Lord's Majesty

"For we did not follow cleverly devised stories when we told you about the coming of our Lord Jesus Christ in power, but we were eyewitnesses of His majesty." 2 Peter 1:16 (NIV)

You grow up hearing stories of Jesus Christ your whole life. You've heard testimonies of what Jesus did in the lives of others, but it makes a huge difference when you actually experience Jesus for yourself. There is nothing like feeling the power of Jesus working in your life. Once you experience Jesus, no one can make you doubt Him. There is nothing in the world like experiencing the power and majesty of the Most High. After experiencing God's love, you realize that you can do all things through Him. There is nothing that scares you after having a true experience with Your Father in Heaven.

OCTOBER 24TH

The Love Of Money

———◈———

"For the love of money is a root of all kinds of evil. Some people, eager for money, have wandered from the faith and pierced themselves with many griefs." 1 Timothy 6:10 (NIV)

There is nothing wrong with having abundance in your life, but money can't be your first priority. Your focus needs to be on God and the purpose you were created for in Christ. Allow God to walk with you through every step no matter how much longer it may take to obtain prosperity. If you focus on fast money and lose focus on God, Satan will deceive you. The money you focused on will become your main worry on earth, destroying you. Your spirit slowly loses its purpose in this world and loses its way toward Heaven. Keep God as your focus and abundance will eventually follow in God's perfect timing.

The Righteous Will Rise Again

———◆———

"Do not lurk like a thief near the house of the righteous, do not plunder their dwelling place; for though the righteous fall seven times, they rise again, but the wicked stumble when calamity strikes." Proverbs 24:15-17 (NIV)

When you're a child of the Most High, the wicked may rise against you, but they won't win the victory over you. God keeps you protected underneath His wings always and He won't allow anyone or anything to take away the position that He gave you in His kingdom. You may fall at times in your life, but you won't stay down forever. When you rise this time, you will be stronger and wiser than you were before your fall. Calamity falls on the wicked, not the righteous. Remain faithful and focused on your Heavenly Father. He is who holds you up always!

Your Flesh Have Been Crucified

———◆———

"And those who are Christ's have crucified the flesh with its passions and desires." Galatians 5:24 (NKJV)

You are becoming the person God created you to be since the beginning of time. Becoming more like Christ is a long, but necessary process. You can't receive all God has for you if you follow your flesh. Your flesh will lead you down dark roads. As you are learning God's Word and walking with Him, He downloads information within you through the Holy Spirit. The Holy Spirit is leading you to freedom, love, light, and power to do all you were created to do here on earth. The first step in becoming all God created you to be is to let go of your fleshly desires and passions. You may stumble at times, but continue walking on as you grow and learn from your past mistakes.

OCTOBER 27TH

Do Not Be Quarrelsome

"And the Lord's servant must not be quarrelsome but must be kind to everyone, able to teach, not resentful. Opponents must be gently instructed, in the hope that God will grant them repentance leading them to a knowledge of the truth, and that they will come to their senses and escape from the trap of the devil, who has taken them captive to do his will." 2 Timothy 2:24-26 (NIV)

God chose you to be a servant to His people. He chose you to teach His truth to others. Be gentle in the way you teach others and be patient with them. Ask God to lead you through His Holy Spirit as you teach others. Keep from falling into anger or arguments. Anger only pushes the person further away from truth. Speak in love and remain in peace. Gently instruct them back into the Word of God.

OCTOBER 28TH

Power, Love, And A Sound Mind

———⊰◆⊱———

"For God hath not given us the spirit of fear; but of power, and of love, and of a sound mind." 2 Timothy 1:7 (KJV)

Once you choose to accept Jesus, you receive His Holy Spirit which teaches you about all things. The Holy Spirit reveals your purpose to you. There will be challenges along the way, but fear not because God is covering you. He chose to fill you with His power to do all He created you to do. Fear is the opposite of love. You are to fear no man, but to love them all. There will be tests along the way that make you feel like you're losing your mind, but continue to pray and trust God to bring you through it all. God blesses His children with perfect peace and sound minds. Hold on through this next battle and trust God to bring you through to the next level.

God's Special Possession

———◆◆◆———

"But you are a chosen people, a royal priesthood, a holy nation, God's special possession, that you may declare the praises of Him who called you out of darkness into His wonderful light."
1 Peter 2:9 (NIV)

God chose you and set His seal on you. You are His. He set you apart to fill you with His Holy Spirit and to use you for a special purpose. When you were lost in darkness, God came to you at your lowest point and brought you into His light. God allows His children to experience a love, peace, and joy that can't be explained. His love is so amazing that there are no words to describe it. He reveals the secret things to you and He draws out the treasures within you as you grow closer to Him. Be forever grateful that God set you here on this earth to achieve greatness.

Only God Can Kill The Soul

"Do not be afraid of those who kill the body but cannot kill the soul. Rather, be afraid of the One who can destroy both soul and body in hell." Matthew 10:28 (NIV)

As a child of God, you're instructed by the Holy Spirit. When you're being led by the Holy Spirit, don't be afraid of what any man thinks or says. You have to do what God is leading you to do. God is the only One who can kill both your body and soul. He is the only One you should fear. Allow the Holy Spirit to guide you in everything since God is the One who created you and raised you up for a time such as this. He created you for a specific purpose for this very time. Ask Him what He wants you to do right now and do not fear what anyone else is feeling, thinking, or saying. You are God's child, not theirs.

God Blesses The Righteous

—◆—

"But even if you should suffer for what is right, you are blessed. 'Do not fear their threats ; do not be frightened.'" 1 Peter 3:14 (NIV)

As you're walking with Christ, your faith is tested. You will experience situations that tell you to either deny Jesus or keep quiet about Jesus. There are times that you are asked to be silent about God and what He's done for you, but this is no time to keep quiet. God has called you to be the salt of the earth. He put you in your situation to bring light and truth to those around you. There is so much going on in this world that indicates the end times are near. This is no time to hide who God put you on earth to be. Speak boldly about your God wherever you are placed. God says whenever you suffer for Him, you are blessed.

NOVEMBER 1ST

Jesus Was The Only Perfect Man

———◆———

"We all stumble in many ways. Anyone who is never at fault in what they say is perfect, able to keep their whole body in check." James 3:2 (NIV)

Following Jesus is an amazing experience. As you are being transformed into the person God created you to be, there will be many obstacles along the way. If you stumble over one of those obstacles, you have to get back up and keep fighting to become who you were meant to be. Jesus was the only perfect man to ever walk this earth. Keep fighting to be more like Jesus and if you trip over any stumbling block, stand back up on your feet ready to try it again. Learn from your fall allowing it to make you stronger and wiser. Your fall is not the end, but it can be the beginning of a whole new life in Christ if you allow it to be.

NOVEMBER 2ND

God Knows Your Faithfulness

"I know your works, tribulation, and poverty (but you are rich); and I know the blasphemy of those who say they are Jews and are not, but are a synagogue of Satan." Revelation 2:9 (NKJV)

God sees everything you do for His Kingdom. He sees how you treat people and love people. He knows what sacrifices you are making for His Kingdom and the suffering you may endure for the Kingdom. God blesses the sacrifices of His children. He rewards them for all they endure for His namesake. God sees how you overcome obstacles placed within your path and He promotes you to the next level if you can persevere through trials that come to test you. Continue growing through the guidance of the Holy Spirit. God sees how much you've grown from the past and He will continue to bless you for the progress you are making daily.

Humble Yourself

---◈---

"For all those who exalt themselves will be humbled, and those who humble themselves will be exalted." Luke 14:11 (NIV)

God gave every one of us different gifts. Your gifts are to help encourage, inspire, uplift, strengthen, teach, unify, and love others around you. Allow the Holy Spirit to draw out your gifts as He moves you wherever He wants you to go and always remember that it is because of God that you're as gifted as you are. Remain humble and be grateful to God for choosing you for the position He's placed you in to help others. Be a great example to the people around you allowing them to see what a true champion looks like. People who are truly gifted don't have to lift themselves up. God will lift you up as you remain humble. Let your gifts speak for themselves.

Jesus Saved You From Death

—◆—

"Now My soul is troubled, and what shall I say? 'Father, save Me from this hour?' No, it was for this very reason I came to this hour. 'Father, glorify Your name!' Then a voice came from Heaven, 'I have glorified it, and will glorify it again.'"
John 12:27-28 (NIV)

Jesus died a horrific death to free you from eternal darkness. His body was beaten and broken for you. He suffered a painful death to give you life. You may be suffering in your own life right now, but remember where you come from. You're a child of the Most High. Your suffering leads to glorification. You come to a crossroads at some point in your life where you can choose light or darkness. You can choose eternal life or death, but you have to choose. What's your choice? Freedom in life or slavery in death?

The Lord Will Fight For You

—————◆————

"Moses answered the people, 'Do not be afraid. Stand firm and you will see the deliverance the LORD will bring you today. The Egyptians you see today you will never see again. The Lord will fight for you; you need only to be still.'" Exodus 14:13-14 (NIV)

Everyone faces battles in their life. You may be fighting a battle with people or a battle within yourself, but don't be afraid. God is stronger than any enemy that rises against you. Whenever you're feeling under attack, remain immovable. Don't allow your feelings of fear to conquer what you know about God. You know the same God who conquered death lives within you. Remain in peace and know that God didn't bring you this far to leave you alone now. After you win this battle, you won't have to fight this enemy again.

God's Child

"The Spirit you received does not make you slaves, so that you live in fear again; rather, the Spirit you received brought about your adoption to sonship. And by Him we cry, 'Abba, Father.'" Romans 8:15 (NIV)

Once you're chosen by God, He dwells within you. He frees you from the ways of the world. You were made free to do all He created you to do. You will still have battles to fight, but you have the Spirit of God living within you. God brought you into His family through the sacrifice Jesus made on the cross. You don't have to continue living as a slave to sin now that you've been set free. Allow yourself to grow through the Holy Spirit as He teaches you about all things. He is who leads you to complete freedom. Now you're free in Christ so there is nothing to fear.

God's Divine Favor

⤙◈⤚

"And the boy Samuel grew in stature, and in favor both with the LORD and with men." 1 Samuel 2:26 (NKJV)

The battle you're facing right now is the gateway to the next dimension. The opposition you're facing today is actually an opportunity. God is pouring out divine favor over you. People who wouldn't normally love you will fall in love with you because of God's plan for your life. When someone who wouldn't normally love you is loving you, praise God because it's a sign that He has opened up the door to the next level. Once you enter the next level, there will always be someone who opposes you, but thank God since you know the enemy always sends someone who hates you whenever you start winning. You have to decide if you want to be liked or if you want to win.

NOVEMBER 8TH

Do Not Turn To Folly

"I will listen to what God the LORD says; He promises peace to His people, His faithful servants— but let them not turn to folly." Psalm 85:8 (NIV)

Difficult times are inescapable for everyone, but these are the times you grow the most. You learn more in the times you want to run and hide from all life is throwing at you. Be willing to listen to what God says if you want to remain in perfect peace. You will still face battles, but the Lord will fill you with a peace which surpasses all understanding. Remain faithful to God no matter what life throws at you. Once God blesses you for your faithfulness, don't turn back to your old ways. God won't throw you away once you've accepted Him into your heart, but you will still have to pay the consequences for any foolishness.

God Understands How You Feel

———◆◇◆———

"For this reason He had to be made like them, fully human in every way, in order that He might become a merciful and faithful High Priest in service to God, and that He might make atonement for the sins of the people. Because He Himself suffered when He was tempted, He is able to help those who are being tempted." Hebrews 2:17-18 (NIV)

God sent His only Son, Jesus to die for you to live. Jesus was tempted by Satan many times, but He never gave in to any of the temptations. Whenever you are feeling tempted or under attack, take a minute and speak to the One who overcame all the tricks of the enemy. Jesus knows what it's like to suffer, which is why you need to trust Him through every situation as He guides you in your process of becoming better and who you were created to be.

NOVEMBER 10ᵀᴴ

God Appoints Representatives

—◦◆◦—

"Every high priest is selected from among the people and is appointed to represent the people in matters related to God, to offer gifts and sacrifices for sins. He is able to deal gently with those who are ignorant and are going astray, since he himself is subject to weakness." Hebrews 5:1-2 (NIV)

God will choose you while you're still out in the world living how the world lives. He will pull you out from among them and begin molding you. He uses those who are most broken so they can't brag about their works. He uses those who have suffered in their own darkness to help others find their way out of darkness. The chosen people are who God uses to show others who are still lost, where to find light. Be grateful for the suffering you've endured since you're now God's chosen!

Wait Patiently For His Promise

———◆———

"When God made His promise to Abraham, since there was no one greater for Him to swear by, He swore by Himself, saying, 'I will surely bless you and give you many descendants.' And so after waiting patiently, Abraham received what was promised." Hebrews 6:13-15 (NIV)

When God gives you a promise, it takes time to unfold. Anyone who is great, has to first go through a process before they receive the promise. The process can make you want to quit, but the harder times are strengthening you for the promise. It's easy to forget the promises of God when you're struggling, but God can't lie. You may not be where you want to be right now, but everyday you're becoming who God called you to be. Everyday you endure the process, you're another day closer to the promise. Be still!

God Offers Salvation To All

"For the grace of God has appeared that offers salvation to all people." Titus 2:11 (NIV)

There is no one perfect on earth. We all make mistakes at some point in our lives, but we serve a God who is big on second chances. God pours out His grace over His children. He took the punishment you deserve for your sins. If you make a mistake, confess your sin to God and ask for forgiveness. His mercies are new every morning. He knows your heart and He won't leave you to suffer alone. God turns your mess into a message. He saves you from what almost destroyed you and then uses you to help strengthen others for the fight they're facing. God won't make you change your ways, but He gives you the option to continue suffering in darkness or PROSPERING IN LIGHT! What do you choose?

NOVEMBER 13TH

Fearfully And Wonderfully Made

———◇———

"I will praise You, for I am fearfully and wonderfully made; Your works are wonderful; Marvelous are Your works, And that my soul knows very well." Psalm 139:14 (NKJV)

God made you different from everyone else. He has a specific mission for you to accomplish here on earth. You're not like anyone else. Don't be afraid to be exactly who God created you to be. He is molding you for something great. Don't be afraid to be different from everyone else because being different is your superpower. Your uniqueness is what gets you into the places God calls you to go. Don't be influenced by the world. Allow God to grow you into who He meant for you to be. Once you have reached your destination, continue to do what you were doing to get you there in the first place. God made you for this very time for a specific reason.

NOVEMBER 14ᵀᴴ

Do Not Worship Other Gods

—◆—

"Do not forget the covenant I have made with you, and do not worship other gods. Rather, worship the LORD your God; it is He who will deliver you from the hand of all your enemies."
2 Kings 17:38-39 (NIV)

God heard your cries whenever you cried out to Him. He saved you from the darkness. When God brought you into His love and His light, He also brought you into His promise. Once God brings you into new levels, don't forget Him. There will be things or even people who come into your life, but don't be distracted by it all. Anything you put over God will eventually become your god. You will lose all God has for you and have to start all over again. God saved you from your enemies and He will continue to do so, but remain faithful through everything. Put Him first always!

You Have Been Redeemed

———⟨◆⟩———

"For He has rescued us from the dominion of darkness and brought us into the kingdom of the Son He loves, in whom we have redemption, the forgiveness of sins." Colossians 1:13-14 (NIV)

God brought you out of the dark you were hiding in and poured out His grace over you. None of us deserve the favor God gives us. His love is so amazing that there are no words to describe it. There is no greater love than sacrificing your only son who's done nothing wrong. You're forgiven for every sin you've ever committed once you've accepted Christ into your heart. Although you felt like giving up or even dying in the dark God brought you out of, you realize that nothing is wasted. God will use your hardest struggle to bring you into an even greater relevance. God is making your name great!

NOVEMBER 16TH

Faith In What You Cannot See

---◆---

"Now faith is confidence in what we hope for and assurance about what we do not see. This is what the ancients were commended for. By faith we understand that the universe was formed at God's command, so that what is seen was not made out of what was visible." Hebrews 11:1-3 (NIV)

God commanded things to form with His Word. He spoke to a thing and it became what He said. You have the same power living within you. Things won't look the way you hope at first, but by faith walk forward believing God's promise. Trust God when things aren't looking as you imagined them and keep in mind that the process is not always pretty. Keep believing God and His Word. Speak out loud what you are envisioning and continue trusting God to provide all you need to make your dream a reality.

Refrain From Anger

―――◦◇◦―――

"Cease from anger, and forsake wrath: fret not thyself in any wise to do evil." Psalm 37:8 (KJV)

You can be right about a situation, but if you react in anger, it automatically makes you wrong. It's important to have self-control. No one can hear your point when they're fearful of your next move. Instead of reacting in anger toward others, respond in love allowing the other person to relax and able to actually listen to what you have to say. In some cases you will find that you're saying the same thing as the other person, but no one can hear each other if they're both upset and angry. If you aren't in agreement with someone else's opinion or argument, sometimes it's better to agree to disagree while still respecting one another and their opinion. Remain in perfect peace.

Everything Grows In God's Time

———⋄———

"He has made everything beautiful in its time. He has also set eternity in the human heart; yet no one can fathom what God has done from beginning to end." Ecclesiastes 3:11 (NIV)

Life gets difficult at times, but the difficult times are what gives you strength and increases your wisdom. At times you may question God when things aren't going the way you've planned them. You may even wonder how you ended up in certain situations, but remember that all things work together for the good of those who love the Lord and are called according to His purpose. None of us can truly understand His ways, but as God's child, it's crucial to fully trust Him. If God allowed something to happen, it's for good reason. Don't allow yourself to become bitter. Trust God and His plan always.

Promised Crown Of Life

"Blessed is the one who perseveres under trial because, having stood the test, that person will receive the crown of life that the Lord has promised to those who love Him." James 1:12 (NIV)

Whenever you're going through hard times, it's a sign that God has opened a new door. There is always a devil to fight before you enter into the next level, but stand strong through it and God will give you the crown of life. Good leadership skills are a blessing from God. If God can trust you, He will move you up in position allowing you to lead His people. If you fall into wickedness, everything under you will suffer. It's important to remain in God allowing Him to lead through you. The higher up you go, the bigger your devil will be to fight. Maintain self-control in your tests.

NOVEMBER 20ᵀᴴ

The Lord Is Your Helper

———◆———

"So we say with confidence, 'The Lord is my helper; I will not be afraid. What can mere mortals do to me?'" Hebrews 13:6 (NIV)

When you have God on your side, there is nothing or no one to be afraid of. He is living within you and is guiding you through His Holy Spirit. Do not fear anything or anyone since you know He is always with you. God does not leave His children. Even when you are going through tests and you can't hear His voice, you know that He is still there, but He's silent because He's allowing you to take the test. The devil will always have someone in your path to stop you from getting to the promise God gave you, but people are just people. God rules over all things and if He said it's yours, then it's yours. Trust Him to move every enemy out of the way.

Show Hospitality To All People

"Keep on loving one another as brothers and sisters. Do not forget to show hospitality to strangers, for by so doing some people have shown hospitality to angels without knowing it. Continue to remember those in prison as if you were together with them in prison, and those who are mistreated as if you yourselves were suffering." Hebrews 13:1-3 (NIV)

Treat others with love and respect. Treat others the same way you would want them to treat you. You never know when one of God's angels are talking to you. There are people who have made mistakes that led them to bad places, but we've all made mistakes. Don't discard people because of their past. You can learn a lot from people who have fallen, but fought their way back up. These are people who can teach you how to conquer your own battles.

You Will Come Forth As Gold

———◇———

"But He knows the way that I take; when He has tested me, I will come forth as gold." Job 23:10 (NIV)

God created you for a specific time for a specific purpose. It's no mistake that you're living on earth at this very time. As you follow God, things will get more difficult. The closer you get to the promise, the more attack you will experience, but rejoice since you know the testing of your faith is shaping you for God's promise. When gold is refined, it goes through a process. Gold is refined in the fire to remove impurities. We go through a similar process. All of your tests and trials will lead to a better you if you choose to learn from them. God is refining you right now and bringing you forth as pure gold. Afterward, you will receive the promise God has for you.

Resist Satan And He Will Flee

—◦◈◦—

"Submit yourselves, then, to God. Resist the devil, and he will flee from you. Come near to God and He will come near to you. Wash your hands, you sinners, and purify your hearts, you double-minded." James 4:7-8 (NIV)

Satan fights you more when you're closer to God's promise. Satan uses the same tricks over and over. We all have a certain devil that comes back to lead us away from God. If you stand strong while you're being tempted by the enemy, he will go away from you. As you move closer to God, He will move closer to you. He gives you the choice to choose light or darkness, but you have to choose. You can't choose to follow God one day and Satan the next day. Although it gets rough on the journey, be patient in the hard times and God will bless you for your loyalty.

NOVEMBER 24TH

Treat Others Fairly

"Therefore, whatever you want men to do to you, do also to them, for this is the Law and the Prophets." Matthew 7:12 (NKJV)

It's important to treat all people with love and respect no matter what your personal opinion may be toward a specific group of people or person. When you're dealing with other people, talk to them the way you expect someone else to talk to you. If you treat others like they're beneath you, then expect to be treated the same way. No one is above anybody. The only One who can judge is God since He is the Creator of all. When God moves you in a position above others, don't take advantage of the power He's trusting you with. As quick as God gave it to you, it can be taken away just as quick or faster. Be respectful and mindful of all people.

Do Not Fall Into Rage

<hr />

"A fool vents all his feelings, But a wise man holds them back." Proverbs 29:11 (NKJV)

Things are going to happen at times which may upset you or make you angry. People will also upset you, but you have to remain in peace. Allow God to handle these situations for you. He will take care of every enemy that rises against you, but you have to stand still and allow God to fight your battles. As hard as it may seem to remain calm, God can fight your battles so much better than you can. If you allow your anger to lead you, it will only make your situation worse. The best thing to do when you're angry is to stay calm even if it means walking away to take a minute. If you're wronged, God will fight your battle and conquer your enemy. He will never forsake His children.

Do Not Lose Heart

———◆◆◆———

"All this is for your benefit, so that the grace that is reaching more and more people may cause thanksgiving to overflow to the glory of God. Therefore we do not lose heart. Though outwardly we are wasting away, yet inwardly we are being renewed day by day." 2 Corinthians 4:15-16 (NIV)

As human beings, we're not perfect. We make mistakes, but Christ chose to give His life for you to save you from the punishment you deserve for your sins. God pours out His grace over you because Jesus took your sins on Himself. This doesn't mean you won't have consequences for your wrongdoings, but if you confess with your mouth and believe in your heart that Christ is your Lord and Savior, you will receive eternal life. Once you receive Christ into your heart, He renews your spirit.

NOVEMBER 27TH

God's Chosen People

———◈———

"But you are a chosen people, a royal priesthood, a holy nation, God's special possession, that you may declare the praises of Him who called you out of darkness into His wonderful light. Once you were not a people, but now you are the people of God; once you had not received mercy, but now you have received mercy." 1 Peter 2:9-10 (NIV)

When you were living in darkness, God called you into His light. He chose you to be a part of His Royal Family. Before coming to God, you felt abandoned. Now God has given you a second chance. He has given you mercy. Whenever you are feeling down, remember what God has already done for you. He didn't save you just to leave you alone now. The process feels difficult at times, but God is with you in the process leading you to His promise.

Do Not Repay Evil For Evil

"Finally, all of you, be like-minded, be sympathetic, love one another, be compassionate and humble. Do not repay evil with evil or insult with insult. On the contrary, repay evil with blessing, because to this you were called so that you may inherit a blessing." 1 Peter 3:8-9 (NIV)

There may be people in your life who are hurting right now. You don't always realize someone is suffering because on the outside, they seem perfectly fine. If someone lashes out at you, remain humble and calm. Try to be understanding of what the person may be feeling instead of getting angry and lashing back out at them. If someone does something to you out of anger, don't get even with them. Instead, bless the person and God will repay. God will bless you for repaying evil with a blessing.

Wisdom From Heaven Is Pure

———◦◦◦———

"But the wisdom that comes from Heaven is first of all pure; then peace-loving, considerate, submissive, full of mercy and good fruit, impartial and sincere." James 3:17 (NIV)

Whenever you're going through a situation where you have to make a tough decision about something important, turn to God for wisdom. Allow God to lead you in the right direction. All good, pure, and lovely things come from God. You will know when you're being led by the Holy Spirit because you will have perfect peace about a decision you're making. If you're feeling confused, remember confusion is not of God. Submit fully to the Lord's will for your life. As you continue in His Word, He fills you with good fruits such as love, peace, and joy. God is filling you with courage to fight the good fight!

Strength And Restoration

———◆◇◆———

"And the God of all grace, who called you to His eternal glory in Christ, after you have suffered a little while, will Himself restore you and make you strong, firm and steadfast. To Him be the power for ever and ever." Amen. 1 Peter 5:10-11 (NIV)

God is gracious toward His children. As a child of God, you will go through a process before you come into the promise. The process can be difficult and make you feel like quitting at times. Whenever you feel like giving up, remember how Christ suffered for you. In order to come into God's glory, you have to withstand the suffering and then He will promote you to glory. Don't quit because after you've suffered, Christ will restore you and strengthen you. He will wipe away every tear you've cried and bless you with His peace.

The Hour Of God's Judgement

"He said in a loud voice, 'Fear God and give Him glory, because the hour of His judgment has come. Worship Him who made the Heavens, the earth, the sea and the springs of water.'" Revelation 14:7 (NIV)

Look at everything happening in this world. You can see the end times are near. It's important to get your life in order because no one knows what day the Lord is coming back. Love God with all your heart and follow Him. Allow Him to lead you through His Holy Spirit. He will lead you to victory and protect you from your enemies. If you stumble, don't move further from God. He is right here helping you back to your feet. He is a very loving and forgiving God. He will never leave you. Remain close to Him. He will be back soon to get His children. Stay ready for His return.

DECEMBER 2ND

God Appointed You

———◆———

"Before I formed you in the womb I knew you, before you were born I set you apart; I appointed you as a prophet to the nations." Jeremiah 1:5 (NIV)

God knew you from the beginning of time. He knew you before your mother and father ever met you. He created you with His hands for a special purpose here on earth. You are set apart from everyone else on earth to accomplish a great mission. It's important to remain close to God because He is your Creator. It only makes sense to ask the Potter what He has created you for. You're uniquely made by God. He knows how many hairs are on your head at this very moment. There is no one else in the world like you. Don't be like everyone else around you because God made you for a specific reason. Ask God to reveal your purpose to you.

DECEMBER 3RD

God Blesses Perseverance

"So do not throw away your confidence; it will be richly rewarded. You need to persevere so that when you have done the will of God, you will receive what He has promised." Hebrews 10:35-36 (NIV)

Instead of playing life safe, take a chance at doing what you love trusting God to bring you into a place of true success and happiness. Go after your purpose with your whole heart and trust God to provide all you need as you chase your dreams. God will reward you for accomplishing your mission on earth. Remain confident in your purpose no matter what others may think or say. Your need for everyone else's acceptance will eventually make you invisible in this world. If you stumble, it's not too late to press the reset button and start over. Don't be afraid to reinvent yourself.

DECEMBER 4ᵀᴴ

Jesus Is Your Rock

———◆◆◆———

"The rain came down, the streams rose, and the winds blew and beat against that house; yet it did not fall, because it had its foundation on the rock. But everyone who hears these words of Mine and does not put them into practice is like a foolish man who built his house on sand. The rain came down, the streams rose, and the winds blew and beat against that house, and it fell with a great crash." Matthew 7:25-27 (NIV)

You can't avoid the storms that life brings. You can't go around it, you have to go through it. You're not a child of God because He stops the storms from rising against you. Everyone goes through storms, but you will know you are God's child when the storms can't stop you. You are God's child when you can take the storms and use them to your advantage.

There Is No Correcting God

——◆——

"Moreover the LORD answered Job, and said, 'Shall he that contendeth with the Almighty instruct Him? He that reproveth God, let him answer it.'" Job 40:1-2 (KJV)

Life can get difficult, especially when you lose people you love. It makes you question God at times when you don't understand why certain things are happening, but God created the Heavens and the earth. He created your story. God works all things for the good of those who love Him. It takes certain hurts and losses to bring you into God's purpose. There are circumstances that come about that are so painful, but God paints a bigger picture that you don't always understand when you're in the midst of a storm. Don't trust your feelings when the storms come. Trust God's Word and remember that these storms will lead you to victory in the end.

DECEMBER 6TH

God Is Slow To Anger

―――◆◇◆―――

"The LORD is slow to anger and great in power, And will not at all acquit the wicked. The Lord has His way in the whirlwind and in the storm, And the clouds are the dust of His feet." Nahum 1:3 (NKJV)

We serve a very loving, merciful, gracious, and forgiving God. Whenever one of His children goes astray, He does not abandon them. God gives you many chances to repent for your sins. He will forgive you, but you still have to suffer the consequences of your actions. If there is no consequence, how will you learn from your mistakes? Although you will have consequences for certain choices you make, God will be with you through it all. God disciplines those He loves. If you backslide, come back to the Lord. Admit your sins to Him and continue in His way. His way will bring you victory!

DECEMBER 7ᵀᴴ

Confess Your Sins To The Lord

———◆◆◆———

"If we confess our sins, He is faithful and just and will forgive us our sins and purify us from all unrighteousness. If we claim we have not sinned, we make Him out to be a liar and His word is not in us." 1 John 1:9-10 (NIV)

As human beings, none of us are perfect. We will make mistakes at times, but it's not the end of the world. There is no one walking this earth who has not sinned at some point in their lives. If you sin, admit your sin so you can be forgiven. If you hide your sins, it will only get worse. Be honest with yourself and God so He can cleanse you from unrighteousness. Don't lie to yourself and make up excuses for your wrongdoings. All people have sinned in some way against God's Word. You can't get better or purified if you won't tell the whole truth.

DECEMBER 8TH

God Blesses Your Sacrifices

"The King will reply, 'Truly I tell you, whatever you did for one of the least of these brothers and sisters of Mine, you did for Me." Matthew 25:40 (NIV)

If you take a good look at the world around you, there are many people suffering who need help. God saved you to use you as a vessel to help others who are in need. God loves it when His children sacrifice for His Kingdom. There are many ways to sacrifice for God's Kingdom like praying with others, ministering to others, spending time with others, or providing for those who are in need. If you're being led by the Holy Spirit to help someone who is struggling, follow that feeling within you to help them. God rewards those who sacrifice for the Kingdom and He promotes those He can truly trust to follow His direction.

DECEMBER 9TH

God's Plan Will Stand

⋙◆⋘

"I know that you can do all everything; And that no purpose of Yours can be withheld from You." Job 42:2 (NKJV)

If you're walking in your true purpose, God will make things work for you. God will move your enemies out of the way, but be careful of playing a certain role in life without the guidance of the Holy Spirit. If the light shining on you is brighter than the light shining within you, it will destroy you. God put you on this earth and He put a certain purpose within you. Walk in your purpose without overthinking things too much. Walk in your purpose with humility, confidence, and power. When you overthink things, it takes away your ability to truly enjoy life. If you live in fear, you will never see the true beauty of life. Push past your fears to accomplish greatness here on earth.

DECEMBER 10TH

Love With Action and In Truth

———❖———

"Dear children, let us not love with words or speech but with actions and in truth. This is how we know that we belong to the Truth and how we set our hearts at rest in His presence: If our hearts condemn us, we know that God is greater than our hearts, and He knows everything." 1 John 3:18-20 (NIV)

Everyone feels good when someone tells them they love them or compliments them, but words are just words. Be careful not to fall into someone's trap because of the smooth words they may use. What kind of action are they putting behind those words? Anyone can speak good things, but pay attention to the way they treat you. God knows all things. If you are feeling condemned about the way you are treating someone or the way they are treating you, it's time to make some changes.

DECEMBER 11TH

Love God And Others

———◆———

"Whoever claims to love God yet hates a brother or sister is a liar. For whoever does not love their brother and sister, whom they have seen, cannot love God, whom they have not seen. And He has given us this command: Anyone who loves God must also love their brother and sister." 1 John 4:20-21 (NIV)

God is love. You may not agree with a person's lifestyle, but your job is to love, not to judge. Loving all people is the commandment God gives His children. Your love toward another person could actually transform their life. Love conquers all. Do some soul searching. If there is hate in your heart, look deep down within yourself and discover where the hate is coming from. Hate is born out of fear. What is the biggest fear you have if you love someone who is not like you?

DECEMBER 12TH

God Answers Prayers

―――――◆◆◆―――――

"This is the confidence we have in approaching God: that if we ask anything according to His will, He hears us. And if we know that He hears us—whatever we ask—we know that we have what we asked of Him." 1 John 5:14-15 (NIV)

You are far more blessed than you may realize at times. The cares of this world can be stressful, but God protects His children. He blesses us with whatever we ask for according to His will. If you're walking in God's purpose, you can ask Him for anything. He hears the prayers of the righteous and they don't go unanswered. Pray to God with confidence and wait patiently. Things will not always look the way you would like them to right away. Don't be deceived by what you see and hear. Believe strongly what you know to be true. Trust God's Word fully.

Jesus Is The True Light

"The True Light that gives light to everyone was coming into the world. He was in the world, and though the world was made through Him, the world did not recognize Him." John 1:9-10 (NIV)

God sent His only Son, Jesus to save you from your sins and free you from the darkness of this world. When Jesus came into the world, He was persecuted because no one recognized Him to be God in the flesh. People still don't recognize Jesus as God in the flesh, but be careful not to be deceived by any man. God's Holy Spirit lives within the lives of those who confess with their mouth and believes in their heart that Jesus is God. He died to free you from your sins and give you access to the Father. God's Holy Spirit continues to intervene within the lives of those who truly love Him.

DECEMBER 14TH

God Blesses Your Descendants

———◆———

"I will surely bless you and make your descendants as numerous as the stars in the sky and as the sand on the seashore. Your descendants will take possession of the cities of their enemies, and through your offspring all nations on earth will be blessed, because you have obeyed Me." Genesis 22:17-18 (NIV)

God loves to bless us with abundance, but we have to follow His lead no matter how difficult things may get. God is using you to break generational curses off your family. Obey God and He will prosper you. Things you suffered as a child will not affect your children and their children. God chose you to bring your family out of darkness and poverty. The choices you make right now will affect the generations coming after you so use wisdom while making life decisions.

DECEMBER 15TH

Be Still, God Will Fight For You

"The Lord will fight for you; you need only to be still."
Exodus 14:14 (NIV)

If you're lying down feeling sorry for yourself, it's time to get up and fight. Don't blame the people around you who are trying to help. People can only do so much to help you. You have to be a part of your own rescue. You have two choices when you are down. You can either lie down and die or you can choose to be a soldier by getting up to fight for your life. You are so much stronger than you realize. The moment you choose to fight, the enemy will do everything he can to keep you down. Remember that the enemy fights you harder when you're closer to your purpose. Trust God, stand up, and be still. The Lord will fight for you. Remember the bigger the battle is, the bigger your blessing will be.

DECEMBER 16TH

Serve The Lord Faithfully

—⊰◆⊱—

"Only fear the LORD, and serve Him in truth with all your heart: for consider how great things He hath done for you." 1 Samuel 12:24 (KJV)

Look back over your life and think about how far you've come. God protected you in ways you don't realize. He allowed you to suffer through things so you could see His power. Your suffering wasn't in vain. He used your struggle to strengthen you for your destiny. He saved you out of darkness to help bring others into His light. Show your gratitude for all He's done for you. Allow Him to use you to help others who are still suffering. This is not about your plan, but about God's plan. God wants to use you for something mighty, but God can use anybody to accomplish His mission so be sure to answer God's call when He calls out to you.

DECEMBER 17TH

Keep Pressing On

"Brothers and sisters, I do not consider myself yet to have taken hold of it. But one thing I do: Forgetting what is behind and straining toward what is ahead, I press on toward the goal to win the prize for which God has called me Heavenward in Christ Jesus." Philippians 3:13-14 (NIV)

There is no one walking this earth who is perfect. We've all made mistakes at some point in our lives. Stop allowing your guilt from the past to control you in this present moment. Keep moving forward. God is with you every step of the way. Open your heart to His Word allowing His power to work through you as He prospers you. God loves to reward you for your sacrifices. You're being strengthened for your purpose. Allow God to clean you up and strengthen you for your position in the Kingdom.

DECEMBER 18TH

Sing Praises To The Lord

"I will praise the LORD according to His righteousness: and will sing praise to the name of the LORD Most High." Psalm 7:17 (KJV)

As God's child, it's important to have an attitude of gratitude in everything you do. When things aren't going the way you would like them to go, continue to be thankful for all God has already done for you. It's hard to be sad or discouraged when you start your day with gratitude. God loves it when He hears His children praise Him. Your praises will break off any spirits of depression. The next time you're feeling down or discouraged, start praising and thanking God for whatever it is that you're asking the Lord to do in your life. When you praise God, the devil will have to flee. Remain confident in the Lord. Walk in your purpose.

Be Merciful To The Doubtful

"Be merciful to those who doubt; save others by snatching them from the fire; to others show mercy, mixed with fear—hating even the clothing stained by corrupted flesh." Jude 1:22-23 (NIV)

There are many people still suffering in darkness. Some of them have heard of Jesus and His love, but there are others who have never heard or experienced the love of Christ. God has shown you great mercy in many of your situations. Be willing to show others the same kind of mercy you've received. Minister to others in love without any kind of judgement. There are different tactics we can use as God's children to introduce others to God's Word and love. It all depends on the person. The Holy Spirit will guide you as you allow God to use you as a vessel to bring others into His light.

DECEMBER 20TH

Remain Calm In All Situations

"A hot-tempered person stirs up conflict, but the one who is patient calms a quarrel." Proverbs 15:18 (NIV)

There are people or situations that may upset you, but there are ways to approach every situation. If someone hurts you or upsets you, it's important to remain calm and in self-control. The moment you react in anger, the other person automatically seems right. Your anger causes you to look as if you are the problem and takes the focus off the real issues. Practice patience in all you do, especially when it comes to situations involving others. Your actions affect everyone involved. If you are right about a situation, God fights for you. The truth will always come to light. The next time you are being tested, remain calm. Don't react in anger, but respond in love.

Meditate On The Lord's Law

———◇———

"Blessed is the one who does not walk in step with the wicked or stand in the way that sinners take or sit in the company of mockers, but whose delight is in the law of the Lord, and who meditates on His law day and night." Psalm 1:1-2 (NIV)

Everyone who crosses your path isn't good for you. It's important to allow God to lead you as He reveals these people to you. Study His Word daily so you aren't easily deceived by the enemy. If God reveals the enemy to you, listen to His guidance. Remove yourself from people who aren't of God. It's important to reach out to all people because you may be the vessel God's using to transform them from their wicked ways, but don't sit in or walk in their ways. Allow God's love to influence them through you and not the other way around.

DECEMBER 22ND

Cast Your Cares On The Lord

———◆———

"Humble yourselves, therefore, under God's mighty hand, that He may lift you up in due time. Cast all your anxiety on Him because He cares for you." 1 Peter 5:6-7 (NIV)

Come humbly to the Lord. Come to Him as a fool because if you come to Him with pride or in your own wisdom, it's hard for you to receive His wisdom. Let go of all you think you know and allow God to lead you. God exalts those who humble themselves before Him. As God lifts you into new heights, it can feel overwhelming. It may cause a little anxiety, but God has His hand on you. Anytime you're moving into higher levels, it will always feel a little scary at first. A lot of us fear the unknown. This is a great reason to remain close to the Lord. Allow the Lord to lead you as He lifts you into new heights.

The Lord Lifts Your Head High

———◈———

"Lord, how many are my foes! How many rise up against me! Many are saying of me, 'God will not deliver him.' But You, Lord, are a shield around me, my glory, the One who lifts my head high." Psalm 3:1-3 (NIV)

The closer you get to your purpose, the more enemies come to surround you. Don't be afraid when people or circumstances come up against you. Get excited because your enemies are a sign that you're closer to your purpose. God surrounds all who surrounds you. He is your protector. God will bring glory out of your suffering and your painful struggles. He loves to show His might in the lives of His children. If you're afraid or feeling really down, don't be discouraged. God is lifting your head right now, wiping away your tears, and filling you with His perfect peace.

DECEMBER 24TH

Dwell In The Safety Of The Lord

"Fill my heart with joy when their grain and new wine abound. In peace I will lie down and sleep, for You alone, Lord, make me dwell in safety." Psalm 4:7-8 (NIV)

The joy of the Lord is your strength. If your outward circumstances aren't looking as you predicted, your inward joy will keep you strong enough to deal with the outside circumstances. You can still have true joy if you abide in God's Word. Trust the Lord as He moves things out of your way to bring you into a place of true success. Don't allow the outward appearance of your situation to discourage you. Things won't look the way you'd like right away because the process is never as pretty as the promise. God is filling you with perfect peace about your situation and He will lay you down tonight with a sound mind.

DECEMBER 25TH

The Lord Forgives You

"Then Peter came to Jesus and asked, 'Lord, how many times shall I forgive my brother or sister who sins against me? Up to seven times?' Jesus answered, 'I tell you, not seven times, but seventy-seven times.'" Matthew 18:21-22 (NIV)

People will hurt you along the way intentionally or unintentionally. As God's child, you're to forgive someone who hurts you no matter how many times they hurt you. Forgiving someone doesn't mean you allow the other person to cross your boundaries. You can forgive someone while still protecting yourself. Forgiveness is not for the other person, it's for you. When you forgive someone who hurt you, it releases you from bitterness and anger allowing you to remain in peace. There is no need to get revenge because God will avenge you in the end.

DECEMBER 26ᵀᴴ

The Lord's Favor Is On You

"For You, O Lord, will bless the righteous; With favor You will surround him as with a shield." Psalm 5:12 (NKJV)

God pours out His favor over His children. He blesses the righteous. He is blessing you right now as you follow His guidance. He blesses whatever your hands touch and wherever your feet walk. As He opens doors for you, trust His hand to hold you up and guide you. Trust Him to provide all you need as you run after your purpose. God covers you with His shield keeping your enemies from touching you. He has a hedge of protection around you that no enemy can penetrate. As long as you remain in Him, God will continue to bless all you do and protect you. Thank God continuously for the favor He has poured out over you and for the access He has given you to His Kingdom.

DECEMBER 27ᵀᴴ

Seek The Kingdom Of God First

"But seek ye first the Kingdom of God, and His righteousness; and all these things shall be added unto you." Matthew 6:33 (KJV)

It is important to learn God's Word daily. As you follow God's instructions and learn His ways, you will begin to want the same things God wants for you. This is why it is so important to follow God's commands as He guides you. Once you receive Christ into your heart, God leads you through His Holy Spirit. When you pray, always ask God for His will to be done. As you grow in Christ, God will bless you with the desires of your heart. He will provide all you need to accomplish His good and perfect will for your life. God blesses His children with prosperity and abundance as they follow His ways. Receive Christ, learn God's Word, and enjoy God's favor.

DECEMBER 28ᵀᴴ

What Is Love?

"Love is patient, love is kind. It does not envy, it does not boast, it is not proud. It does not dishonor others, it is not self-seeking, it is not easily angered, it keeps no record of wrongs."
1 Corinthians 13:4-5 (NIV)

God puts people in your path that He wants you to reach out to in love. Your love could be the very thing that transforms an individual and brings them closer to God. It's important to remain calm and patient when interacting with others so they're able to experience God's love through you. Allow God to use you as a vessel to love, strengthen, encourage, and inspire others to be the person they were created to be on earth. If someone hurts you, don't get even. Continue to love the person with everything you got. Show them what true love is all about.

Jesus Is The Living Stone

———❖———

"As you come to Him, the Living Stone—rejected by humans but chosen by God and precious to Him— you also, like living stones, are being built into a spiritual house to be a holy priesthood, offering spiritual sacrifices acceptable to God through Jesus Christ." 1 Peter 2:4-5 (NIV)

As a follower of Christ, you will suffer rejection like Jesus did by His own people. How well you handle rejection determines how far you go as you fight to complete your mission. Your faith will be tested as you pursue your purpose. Can you handle rejection and continue walking forward by faith? God allows you to be tested before moving you to the next level. Jesus was also rejected, but He continued on His mission. Are you able to move forward after being rejected to accomplish your mission?

God Will Not Make You Go Alone

"And the Lord said to Joshua, 'Today I will begin to exalt you in the eyes of all Israel, so they may know that I am with you as I was with Moses.'" Joshua 3:7 (NIV)

God uses others to inspire you, but He doesn't want you to emulate them. There is nothing wrong with being inspired by other people, but God made you with uniqueness. Be inspired by others without cloning their style. God set you apart for a reason. Love who God created you to be. God chose you to accomplish a mission different from anyone else on this earth. Enjoy being different and unique. God didn't call you to be your idol, He called you to achieve greatness while being yourself. God only promised to be with You like He was with the great people He called before you, but you are a designer's original!

DECEMBER 31ST

Do Not Be Easily Provoked

———◆———

"Be not hasty in thy spirit to be angry: for anger resteth in the bosom of fools." Ecclesiastes 7:9 (KJV)

There will be different tests along the way as you continue on your journey. Be careful from allowing different tests or people to drive you to anger. When you become angry in your spirit, don't allow the anger to control what you say to others or what you do to others. Your anger can take over you if you allow it and make your situation worse than it is already. It's important to learn how to transform your anger into fuel for your journey. If something or someone upsets you, take a minute to breathe and use your anger to motivate you to reach for better. You don't have to get revenge. All you have to do is keep accomplishing greatness and allow God to avenge you.

Printed in the United States
By Bookmasters